Roadmaps To Freedom™ Series
Personal Transformation That Sticks

Emotional Freedom From COVID-19

How to Stop the Overwhelm . . . Build a New Life . . .
And Beat the Odds!

Kathy E. Williamson

Copyright © 2021 by Kathy E. Williamson

All rights reserved. No part of this publication may be reproduced, distributed, or transmitted in any form or by any means, including photocopying, recording, or other electronic or mechanical methods, without the prior written permission of the publisher, except in the case of brief quotations embodied in critical reviews and certain other non-commercial uses permitted by copyright law.

This publication is designed to provide competent and reliable information regarding the subject matter covered. However, it is sold with the understanding that the author and publisher are not engaged in rendering medical, legal, financial, accounting, or other professional advice. Laws and practices often vary from state to state and if medical, legal, financial, or other expert assistance is required, the services of a professional should be sought. The author and publisher specifically disclaim any liability that is incurred from the use or application of the contents of this book.

All Scripture quotations, unless otherwise indicated, are taken from the Holy Bible, New International Version*, NIV*. Copyright ©1973, 1978, 1984, 2011 by Biblica, Inc. Used by permission of Zondervan. All rights reserved worldwide. www.zondervan.com. The "NIV" and "New International Version" are trademarks registered in the United States Patent and Trademark Office by Biblica, Inc.

EMOTIONAL FREEDOM FROM COVID-19; HOW TO STOP THE OVERWHELM ... BUILD A NEW LIFE ... AND BEAT THE ODDS!

Daily Growth Publishing
www.DailyGrowthPublishing.com
Support@DailyGrowthPublishing.com

Ordering Information for Quantity Purchases

Special discounts are available on quantity purchases. Contact the publisher.

Printed in the United States of America
1st Edition January 2021
ISBN: 978-1-7363883-0-3 (paperback)
ISBN: 978-1-7363883-1-0 (ebook)

Other Books by Kathy E. Williamson

My Friend Is an Addict – What Can I Do? Use the Roadmap Out of Addiction To Influence Your Friend And To Take Back Your Life

Tapping Away Your Addiction: Freedom and Confidence in Yourself Await You

* * * * * * *

Free 30 page PDF ebook

The sections of the book you are reading relating to the skill of Tapping have been pulled together into this 30 page PDF ebook. It is also available on Amazon as a Kindle ebook. Both formats can easily be loaded to your cell phone for quick access in your moment of need.

For your free PDF copy go to:
www.EmotionalFreedomFromCOVID19.com/freeguide

Dedication

This book is dedicated in memory of my dear friend Andrea Nelson. It was during the time leading up to her passing away (during the COVID pandemic) that the Lord gave me the idea to write this book. The overwhelming grief I felt was finally relieved when I personally applied the process taught in this book. Although I know I will see Andrea in heaven when I get there, I did not want her life of laughter and love to go unrecognized here on earth. And that even her passing influenced one person to write a book that will impact thousands of lives.

* * * * * * *

Praise be to the God and Father of our Lord Jesus Christ, the Father of compassion and the God of all comfort, who comforts us in all our troubles, so that we can comfort those in any trouble with the comfort we ourselves receive from God.

2 Corinthians 1:3-4 (NIV)

Table Of Contents

Introduction 1

Chapter 1: Preparation For The Journey 5

Chapter 2: Choose My Destination 13

Chapter 3: Change My Focus 21

Chapter 4: Control My Emotions 27

Chapter 5: Challenge My Beliefs 35

Chapter 6: Clarify Underlying Issues 47

Chapter 7: Communicate With Purpose............................ 55

Chapter 8: Change My Lifestyle 67

Chapter 9: Faith, Hope And Love 73

Chapter 10: How To Build A New Life 81

Chapter 11: Daily Rituals For A New You 91

Chapter 12: Words Of Encouragement 93

Appendix A: Tapping Into Peace 95

Appendix B: Forgiveness Brings Freedom 121

Appendix C: Discover Your Passion 129

Appendix D: Daily Rituals 139

Appendix E: Resources 141

Introduction

This is a new era in our world where our emotional turmoil has deepened because of so many factors out of our control. Thousands of people worldwide have lost a loved one during this pandemic. Losing your loved one to death during this COVID-19 season presents more problems than if the person died prior to this period of chaos. Whether your family member or friend died from COVID-19 or other reasons, the grieving process entails more emotions than normal. Why?

During a time of isolation due to the pandemic, all our lives were disrupted. Having to stay home and lose interaction with others has led to anger, bitterness, pent-up emotions, and for many, a state of hopelessness and fear. Being unable to be with our loved one while he or she was sick and dying left us unable to be their advocate and also share our love with them. The power of touch was stripped away.

Grief is now intensified and fuels our daily living with additional unwanted feelings that we no longer know how to cope with. This pandemic is the first (and hopefully the only) one to happen during our lifetime. For the first time we are facing an unknown future, leaving us feeling like we have no control over our lives and our impact on helping others.

Is it possible to move on when our lives have been

disrupted in so many areas? Yes. My hopes are to show you a roadmap to get you from where you are to a better and brighter future. While you may feel the odds are against you for getting through this successfully, the end results are within your power and it is possible to rise above the odds.

Besides grieving over the death of a loved one, many other losses may be playing havoc on our emotions. Things such as loss of financial income, loss of social interaction, loss of family gatherings, loss of a picture for a bright future, loss of control in many situations, loss of speed in forging ahead in our careers, and many other types of losses.

This book is written during the pandemic and therefore I do not have answers as to how society will continue to change nor the devastating effects of businesses closing and the jobless rate increasing. But I am aware of the mounting emotions that drain us of energy, hope and a positive outlook on life. My ability to lower the intensity of my emotions, especially around the death of a friend (non-COVID-19 related), allowed me to stop the downward spiral of out-of-control emotions.

Previous to this book I had developed my *Roadmaps To Freedom* process which sets forth the *7 C's to Transformation That Sticks*. This process can be applied to overcoming and controlling our emotions during these times of uncertainty during a pandemic.

Below are the *7 C's to Transformation That Sticks*. Each section will be discussed in-depth in this book. To obtain the transformation that you seek, the 7 C's should be followed in sequential order.

1. Choose My Destination
2. Change My Focus
3. Control My Emotions
4. Challenge My Beliefs
5. Clarify Underlying Issues

6. Communicate With Purpose
7. Change My Lifestyle (Habits)

You might wonder how some of the sections could help with the grieving process or stopping our emotional overwhelm. You will learn how our thoughts impact all areas of our lives, especially our emotions. Another proven fact is that a lot of our problems are resolved as a by-product of doing something else. This will become clear as you go through this process.

Each chapter is broken down into four major components:
1. An overview of the problem
2. Your current situation
3. The transformation you seek
4. Knowledge, skills and habits to make transformation possible

This process can be used on various problems which cause emotional turmoil. At times I ask you to review the teaching and then write down your insights around that topic. So keep pen and paper (or a journal) handy as you go through this book.

For a quick start on understanding and implementing the content in this book, watch a video wherein I give the overview of the book. Go to

www.EmotionalFreedomFromCOVID19.com/overview

Chapter 1

Preparation For The Journey

A journey without proper preparation can lead to disasters. ~Kathy Williamson

I just ended a telephone conversation with a friend who advised me that a mutual friend of ours was going to go into hospice. I knew this day was coming, but I still was not ready for it. Although my dying friend had accepted her fate, it was difficult for her family and friends to accept it. We loved her so much and she brightened our lives every time we were around her.

Grief flooded over me in waves that wouldn't quit. I wanted to visit her to say goodbye, but the circumstances wouldn't allow it. I tried to control my emotions the rest of the day, knowing I had to go to work that evening where my job was to listen over the phone to people going through struggles and give them encouragement. I was the one needing encouraging, but no one was available to provide that for me or give me a hug to comfort me. My friend who called could cry with me over the phone, but the encouragement was short-lived.

That evening at work the first call I got was from a lady who lost her dog over the weekend. She was crying uncontrollably, which immediately stirred up my emotions that I tried to stuff during the day. I made it through that call, took a short break, and was able to finish my shift. When I got home late that night, I was a basket case. It had been so long since I felt so overwhelmed by grief.

Then I remembered to try Tapping to release my emotions. (I will teach you this skill in this book.) I wish I could say I always remember to do this, but I don't! So I did some Tapping on the thoughts and emotions I was going through and within half an hour I felt release from the overwhelm. It was such a big relief I couldn't believe I forgot to do the Tapping when my emotions first began to build up.

As I sat on the side of my bed I was in awe at how calm I was—especially after being in emotional turmoil all day and evening. Over the next few days as my grief would tend to build up, I quickly did my Tapping to release it. I was so thankful that I knew about Tapping. Then towards the end of the week I began to think about all the people who have died during the pandemic (either from COVID-19 or unrelated) and how their grief over the death of someone close was compounded due to the circumstances preventing the normal course of saying goodbye to a loved one, holding a funeral, and receiving emotional support from others.

I thought that because Tapping works great and can provide relief in a short span of time, I felt God telling me to let others know about things they can do to relieve their emotional overwhelm during this pandemic. Not just for the grief over the passing of a loved one, but for all the other pent-up emotions that have arisen during this time. Thus this book was written to bring some sort of sanity back into our lives during times of uncertainty.

****

This book is for anyone experiencing any of the following emotional overwhelm due to the COVID-19 pandemic:
- You lost a loved one and the grief is unbearable.
- You are a frontline responder exhausted and stressed.
- Suffering loss of: job, finances, relationships, physical activities, or spiritual connections.
- You are a current (or long-hauler) COVID-19 sufferer who has fears and anxieties about the unknown future.
- Your anger over societal changes imposed upon you rules your life.

A successful journey requires the attainment of knowledge and skills before you start. If you were taking a road trip, you would need to have a map with a route planned out from where you are to where you want to go, knowledge of where you want to stop each night of the trip, how much fuel you will need, the finances necessary, what places you want to visit during the trip, and a possible time frame to do all this in.

Remember as kids how we would be so excited for the vacation our parents were planning? They would get us pictures of the theme park we would visit, or give us mental pictures of how great it was going to be when we arrived. We would pour over those pictures to keep us excited and to motivate us to do whatever was necessary to prepare for the trip.

To map out our personal journey, we also need to gather pictures of the destinations we want to reach. These exciting pictures keep us stirred up emotionally to pull us through difficult circumstances that may arise on our journey. It is so easy to lose our momentum when tough times come. That is why putting together a vision board is so important. Many people scoff at this, but its benefits far outweigh anybody's attack over its validity.

Most vision boards focus on tangible items a person wants to obtain. However, I propose creating a vision board that has more of a focus on character development. Our fulfillment in life comes from our relationships and being the best person we are capable of being. My vision board consists of goals for the next year. I have my top three personal goals and my top three goals on how to reach out to love and help others.

For example, my personal goals are to take a vacation to Southern California, get more involved in making friends through church, and improve my health (I am still recovering from congestive heart failure in early 2019). My goals on how to reach out to love and help others consists of building up my business through the sales of this book you are reading, creating a community of like-minded people who can encourage each other in their growth, and to do a TEDx talk. Intangible things I want to work on for developing my character are to get out into the community more (instead of hiding behind my computer), consistency in everything I do, and to take action daily to implement the steps to lead me to fulfilling the big dreams for my life.

Other people who are not developing businesses may want to focus on finding an avenue to reach out to love and help others. Rather it be through volunteering, forming a group to reach out to specific people, or impacting people by the way you live and your deep relationships with them. Sometimes, instead of finding pictures to reflect these intangible items, I will write the word in large letters on my vision board as a reminder.

I want to emphasize that our main goals should be focused on influencing other people, not focused on how to increase our income and buy more stuff. Yes, our finances will increase as we serve others, but not if we are "chasing" money. This is a major shift I had to make in my life, and it wasn't easy with all the advertisements in our western world on how to get rich. So I encourage you to think about things you want to put on your vision board as you read through this book.

The journey to a brighter future also requires us to have certain knowledge, skills and habits to get us to our anticipated future. In each section of this journey of the *7 C's to Transformation That Sticks*, I set forth what these are. Therefore, it is best to begin our journey by touching base on what these are and a basic understanding of each.

Tapping

The first skill to learn is called Tapping (also known as EFT, short for Emotional Freedom Technique). This is a simple five-minute technique for reducing overwhelming emotions. Tapping has helped many people who have been stuck for years in painful memories, fears, anxieties, insecurities, and even physical pain. It also helps with reducing new negative emotions before they become overwhelming. A more detailed explanation of this skill is set forth in Appendix A. I suggest you read it now before proceeding with the rest of this chapter.

When I went through the grief over my friend as discussed above, the Tapping totally improved my emotional state. It did not make me deny what was happening, nor diminish the effect of losing her, but getting my emotional state under control allowed me to move on with my daily activities without constantly feeling overwhelmed. Although I have used Tapping on numerous areas of my life, this time it had its greatest impact on lowering my emotional state.

Attention COVID-19 Frontliners: A special section for you and your unique stresses is in Appendix A. I suggest you read that section first for immediate relief and hope.

Appendix A has been turned into a free PDF ebook: *Tapping Into Peace and Hope Amid COVID-19: A Better Life Awaits You Today.* This ebook contains excerpts from this book dealing with Tapping on various emotions and issues addressed in this book. This PDF ebook was created for you as a quick reference guide. Go to my website to get your free copy: www.EmotionalFreedomFromCOVID19.com/freeguide. It is also available on Amazon as a Kindle ebook.

Forgiveness

Forgiveness is a major key to being able to overcome grief and loss during this pandemic. Forgiveness sometimes can be an hourly or a daily process. Most people are not taught that once you forgive, you need to commit to never bring up that episode again—either verbally or in your thoughts. Without this step, a person ends up rehashing how they were hurt in their past (even if it was this morning) and how they were done wrong (the victim mentality).

When a person decides to stop this stinking thinking, he or she must have something to replace those thoughts. That is where working daily on building one's vision for an awesome future plays a major role (chapter 3 discusses this). Not only does it provide something positive to think about, but when a person is operating in their passion, it gives so much emotional fuel to keep them headed in the right direction. Pretty soon, we have a reason "not" to stay in our negative emotional turmoil. Our life and outlook are changed as a by-product of working on our dreams.

Are you holding on to anger and hurt from how your grief and/or loss has impacted your life? You may *feel* that you're not ready to forgive. However, you can't let your feelings make decisions for you. This act of forgiveness isn't for the benefit of the person or situation that hurt you, it's for you. If you wait until your feelings tell you it's time to forgive, you will be waiting a long time, as well as wasting a lot of your life that could be lived from a better place of peace and purpose.

Appendix B sets forth more details of this process. I suggest you read it now and ask God to help you apply this information immediately.

Create a New Vision For Your Future

The importance of having an awesome vision for your future is that when you begin to stop focusing on your grief and emotional turmoil, you need something to switch your focus to. This skill is discussed at the beginning of the process because it is integral to have this available while you travel your Roadmap to Freedom. This positive outlook for your future allows you to keep yourself from continuing down the slippery road to emotional overwhelm.

Once again, because this is an in-depth process, it is set forth in Appendix C. I suggest you read it and begin developing your plan for your awesome future. As you read through this book, you may receive further insights on how to build your awesome future.

Now is the time to develop this vision, even though we have no idea what the future "norm" will be for our society. I encourage you to think outside the box about what you want to do, and how to love and impact people with your unique gifts.

CHAPTER 2

CHOOSE MY DESTINATION

> *Without a personal destination for our lives, we allow ourselves to be blown by the winds of change, some we would prefer not to encounter.*
> ~Kathy Williamson

Before you begin any trip you must know where you are starting from and where you want to go. The same holds true if you wish to change things in your life. Although you know you want to get out of the overwhelm of grief and loss, you must have a picture of the state of mind you wish to achieve.

The goal is not to eliminate and dismiss what has happened to you during this pandemic, but to honor what you have gone through yet recover with a better attitude and a hope for a brighter future. We can still honor the person who passed away without having the overwhelming emotions that hinder our moving forward in life. Other losses we experienced through this pandemic can either lead us into a life of hopelessness or we can work on ourselves during this time and determine to beat the odds that are against us and come out stronger.

Where Are You Currently At?

Let's take a look at where you might be at in your life—emotionally, physically, financially, relationships, and spiritually. When we improve one area, the others improve also. Use your journal to write down your current status as we go through each area.

1. Emotionally—Grief Over:

- A loved one who has passed away
- Our inability to physically be with this loved one, to be their advocate, to share our love with them, to be by their side when they passed away—leaving us with a sense of lack of closure to this incident.

2. Emotionally—Anger/Fears Over:

- Loss of a job, financial income, family events, in-person church attendance, birthday parties, school events, children's activities, loss of the world we knew, etc.
- Someone else exercising control over us
- Loss of our freedoms and constitutional rights [However, this may be righteous anger, which is acceptable.]
- Our personal inability to provide for our loved ones
- We cannot immediately "fix" our problems
- The uncertainty of our future

3. Physically—Loss of:

- The power and encouragement from touching another person
- Ability to work out at gyms, play sports, compete in competitions
- Personal space needed for escape and renewal

4. **Health (COVID Sufferers – Current and Long-Haulers)**
   - Intensified fears, being scared, frustrated
   - Isolation, even from others in your household
   - Panic
   - Anxiety
   - Doubts you can handle this

5. **Financial—Loss of:**
   - Ability to make ends meet, even the most common survival needs of food, a roof over our heads, car payments, material necessities of life, and the extra things that make life better, etc.
   - A job, which also entails the loss of comradery among coworkers, chance for personal growth and advancement in your career
   - Savings and/or retirement funds

6. **Relationships—Loss of:**
   - Daily interaction with people outside your immediate family
   - Chances to deepen new relationships due to social distancing
   - Ability to be physically present to love and encourage your family or friends
   - Peace in relationships due to clashes brought on by isolation, emotional overwhelm, and a constantly changing society

7. **Spiritually—Potential Losses:**
   - Unable to gather together in person in a church setting
   - The ability to have close interactions with other Christians and grow spiritually
   - The availability to physically reach out to share the Gospel with people.

- Peace with God—some are blaming God for what's happening, not realizing other factors play into what is occurring in our world.

The resulting negative emotions from this grief and losses include:

- Worry about ourselves and loved ones
- Loss of safety
- Feelings of isolation
- Worries of how to live in this current pandemic
- Fears of what the future does or does not hold
- Sadness over the state of affairs, both personally and throughout societies
- Anger and/or rage over various things
- Holding a grudge against people or circumstances
- A steadfast focus on and verbally rehashing of all the negative stuff going on, which then becomes overwhelming

Now that we have identified some of the predominant negative feelings, let's look at examples of where we might want to go. Our focus is on our emotional state, not necessarily each of the above-listed scenarios.

Where Do You Want To Go?

The grief process and the time it takes to go through it is different for every person. Some may go through it quickly, for others it lasts for years (especially if they do not have the skills taught in this book). Again, our goal is not to forget about our loved ones who passed away nor these things that are happening to us at the moment, but to manage our emotional state which will allow us to not get stuck in this overwhelming frame of mind. Some goals for this emotional overwhelm could be:

- Ease my grief and/or excessive crying
- Somehow be able to express my grief

- Not be overtaken by grief every day
- To be comforted by someone
- Release of my anger and knee-jerk responses
- Back to a normal daily routine with normal emotions
- Instill emotions of hope and positive expectations

A large component that hinders us from moving forward to where we want to go emotionally is the fact that we don't have any idea of how long this pandemic will last, nor its total impact upon the world. The anticipated fear of our future can keep us in a position of feeling stuck. But I want to encourage you that even if this is where you are, you can bring emotional freedom to your current lifestyle. Instead of us wasting our time during these uncertain times, let's take the steps necessary to live in peace no matter what is going on, and to always have a glimpse of hope we can focus on.

Therefore, in order to move forward we must know what knowledge, skills and new habits will get us through this pandemic and prepare us for our future.

Knowledge, Skills & Habits Needed

I trust you have taken the time to read and study the skills discussed in the Appendixes. If not, please take a moment to review them. In each chapter I set forth the items needed to master the transformation addressed in that chapter.

While this section in each chapter is shorter, it is the most important part to learn so you can obtain your emotional freedom from COVID-19.

You may find yourself returning to this chapter to identify the specific emotions that come up as you go through this transformation process.

If you had emotions arise while reading this chapter, you can begin to immediately release them by utilizing the following:

- Tapping – see the examples in Appendix A. By learning this technique first, it helps to relieve any anxieties about moving forward in your life, even in these unknown times of change. Tapping can also be tried regarding physical symptoms. (Although I make no guarantees of a successful resolution of physical problems. The major focus of this book is to obtain freedom from overwhelming emotions.)

- Forgiveness – I am sure you can think of someone who has either personally caused you emotional turmoil, or through their decisions have affected your ability to remain in control of everything in your life. You may not *feel* ready to forgive these people or government officials. And I understand this. I am not asking you to ignore the consequences of what they did, but I am asking you to consider that holding back forgiveness is affecting *you*, not them. The sooner you make the decision to forgive someone, the quicker the flare-ups of your overwhelming emotions will begin to diminish. I ask that you be willing to see the whole picture of how the elements discussed in this book compound each other. Therefore, when you improve one area, the effect carries into all areas of your life.

- Journaling – It will be helpful to grab pen and paper (a journal if you prefer) to record your thoughts as you go through this book. I suggest you go back through the examples given in this chapter and identify the ones that resonate with you, specifically listing the people (or people who have caused the situations) who have hurt you or angered you.

An important aspect of journaling is to add verbal expression of what you are journaling about (speak it out loud after you have written it). If you begin to cry, that's okay. Crying is very healing.

Part of your journaling at this point is to put together your personal Roadmap to Freedom. Go back and choose the items that pertain to you—both in where you currently are and where you want to go. This will give you a starting point for your Roadmap. As you go through each chapter you may find more things to add to this Roadmap, whether it be concrete things or just an emotional state.

Let's move on to learn how having a positive vision for your life, which utilizes your passion in life, can impact every area of your life as a by-product of instituting it.

* * * * * * *

Like so many others, I wanted to quit being financially broke all the time. I knew what I didn't want, but until I had a picture and a plan on what I did want financially, nothing seemed to work to change my situation. And I would emotionally go back into worry, doubt and fear that I wouldn't be able to pay my rent and other bills.

It was so easy to fall back into my mentality of lack and inability to raise my level of income. Every time I had a new vision of how much money I wanted, I would get excited for a little while, make some effort to make things work, but when nothing worked, I would quit. I would end up telling myself, *look at how long you've been trying to raise your income and you haven't! Why would things be different this time? Why waste your efforts trying something you know won't work?* Ever been there yourself?

At a conference I attended for personal development and being successful in business, the biggest two takeaways I had were these:

First, stop getting down on yourself. It is not YOU that's making your efforts fail—it's the systems and processes you don't have in place, or you are using the wrong ones. The right processes for your type of business work, regardless of who uses them! Second, stop chasing money and focus on changing the lives of others. Then money will come.

While the above is true, I also know that my mindset and beliefs that they will work for me also play a large role in being successful. The thing that changed my life was developing Daily Rituals to keep me focused on what I do want to change financially. As a Christian I believe God has given me a vision to help people in their personal transformation so they can live a life filled with love, laughter, and purpose. My faith in that vision is proven by the actions I take to make it so.

It was not easy to make that major shift and keep the right perspective in front of me every day. But as I looked back at God's faithfulness to always provide for me, it helped ease my emotional worries and fears. I also use Tapping to instill a vision of me living a life filled with abundance in all areas of my life.

CHAPTER 3

CHANGE MY FOCUS

> *A life lived unintentionally is a life lived in vain.*
> ~Kathy Williamson

When we take a road trip our focus is on our end destination. We envision ourselves having fun at that theme park or attending our family reunion. Our excitement pushes us through doing some of the things we don't want to do to prepare for the journey, or even have to put up with during the journey. We know the end result will be worth it. You will notice our focus is not on *how can I leave where I'm at (or stop doing what I do)*. In chapter 5 when we discuss changing our beliefs and thoughts, we will discover that what we think about eventually becomes our reality. Therefore, in order to leave our current state of mind, we must have a better vision to think about and have a clear picture of it in our mind. If you have not read Appendix C, *Discover Your Passion*, take a few moments to do so before reading further.

You might wonder what developing a vision for your future does to help your current state of emotional overwhelm. We always have thoughts in our mind. Recently they may have all been focused on the negative things going on in our lives and how we have become so emotionally burdened because of them. We can't just stop those thoughts and not think about anything. We must have something good to turn our thoughts toward. Thus, developing a great vision for our future provides that missing element.

What is Your Current Focus?

Let's take a brief look at some of the things we currently might be focusing on:

- Focused on my grief (over the loss of a person or loss of finances, social interaction, etc.)
- My inability to be with my loved one before and after he/she passed.
- The uncertainty of my future due to COVID-19.
- All I can see is loss after loss after loss. How much more can I take?
- Anticipation of more bad things to happen.
- When will my physical symptoms go away for good?

Once we use the Tapping skill to reduce or get rid of the emotional overwhelm on each of these, then we can take steps to improve our lives for the better.

New Dreams From New Focus

After going through Appendix C and determining what your passion is in life, you now have a solid goal to work on.

However, a lot of people are not able to determine their passion quickly. In fact, the majority of people go through their entire life allowing other people and circumstances to direct their paths. A life lived unintentionally is a life lived in vain. I don't want you to die with your dreams still inside you.

So what do you do if you can't immediately determine

your passion in life? Take a look at what you love to do, even if you can't get paid to do it. Unfortunately, during this pandemic with social distancing required, our physical interactions with others are very limited. However, many things have moved to being conducted over the Internet, which in many cases reaches massive amounts of people we could not reach in our physical outreach. Is there some way you can take your passion and use the Internet to (1) connect with the people you want to help, (2) perhaps provide online teaching for them—either in a free group or a paid membership group, (3) create a Facebook group for them to gather to learn and encourage each other, (4) provide a series of video teachings via YouTube, and other possible avenues.

If your passion is not something you can take online, you can still dream about your vision coming to fruition once the pandemic subsides and personal social interaction resumes. Perhaps you can use this time to write your book and start promoting it.

Here are some new possible emotional states to focus on:

- I accept the losses in my life as real and know it's okay to grieve. I can still grieve without the emotional overwhelm.
- I know a brighter future awaits me where I can use my passion in life to reach out to love and help others.
- I can have deeper relationships because of what I've learned from living through the COVID-19 pandemic.
- I can share what I have learned in this book with my relatives and friends to enable them to take control of their emotions during these trying times.
- I am excited at the possibilities of taking my passion online and helping massive amounts of people.
- Now is the time to work on _____ in my life that I have never had the time to focus on.

- I am going to beat the odds, and totally recover from my run-in with COVID-19!

I CAN, I WILL, WATCH ME!

Knowledge, Skills & Habits Needed

The Tapping skill is used not only to reduce or eliminate emotional issues, it is also used to instill positive emotions about new possibilities for our future. Appendix A sets forth some examples to use for this aspect of your growth.

Per the instructions in Appendix C, begin to shift your focus so that 80% of your thought life and actions focus on building your awesome future, and then spend 20% of your time working on maintaining your emotional stability and/or resolving any underlying issues you may have (see chapter 6 for identifying these issues).

Journaling allows you to write out your hopes and dreams for a brighter future. You can use your words to paint pictures of seeing yourself fulfilling your visions for numerous areas of your life. Reviewing these word pictures daily keeps your mind focused in the right direction and it provides good emotional fuel to keep you from going backwards in life.

From your journaling you can begin to write out a specific plan on ways to make your vision become a reality. Once you know where you want to go, you can backtrack to determine what needs to be done to accomplish it. This is an excellent time to build this plan and get excited for life again. Should your mind want to sabotage you and tell you that you're not good enough, or don't have the education to do it, or that your dreams never come true, use Tapping to counter these thoughts and to replace them with new, positive thoughts that will drive you forward.

Continue to build your vision board. Are there pictures depicting your desires that can be added to your board? Be sure these pictures excite you.

* * * * * * *

In 2019 I had severe congestive heart failure. Mentally it did a number on me. Here I was trotting along in life, believing I was going to live until around 100 years old (my grandmother died at age 99 and my mom at age 93), and then this dire picture of my heart turned my life upside down for a while. I was now faced with the questions of could I get through this, would my heart get much better with medication, and what was now my life expectancy?

This occurred in April, and it wasn't until early fall that I was getting better and could see light at the end of the tunnel and it wasn't a death train. But the months of worrying and being fearful had stopped me cold in the pursuit of my dreams. One day I realized that all of my thoughts and conversations were about my bad health. I needed to change my focus.

I had to stop completely mentioning anything about my bad health to others. After all, didn't I used to get tired of listening to old people talk only about their bad health? It was not easy to stop, and I can't say I have completely done so, since other health problems have creeped up as a result of the medications I am on.

I had to get back to focusing on my dreams again. But this time it was more like, which one(s) could I accomplish in the (little?) time I had left in life? Then as time progressed and I began to feel better and my heart improved tremendously, I began to believe that I can still live to a ripe old age. So I started dreaming BIG again!

I have seen this type of inward focus happen to people who have been hit hard by the pandemic. And this is the same process I wish for them to follow to take back their lives. To change their focus from all the negative outcomes and start dreaming about positive visions for their lives to come to fruition.

Chapter 4

Control My Emotions

> *To regain control of our lives, we must take control of our emotions daily.* ~Kathy Williamson

Emotions lie to us. They deceive us into thinking they are too powerful for us to control. Our negative emotions are based on a lot of lies from our past, which keeps us from moving forward in our lives. For example in chapter 6, *Clarify Underlying Issues*, one issue discussed is not being willing to forgive someone until that person has acknowledged what they did to us or has somehow made amends to us. Our emotions keep us in a frenzy telling us that we can't forgive until they pay for the hurt they caused us. This unforgiveness can lead to bitterness and can also lead to physical ailments. The truth about forgiveness is that the benefit is for you, not the person who harmed you.

As a Christian I try to follow God's example where He forgives us *immediately* once we repent and ask Him to, and He also remembers it no more. Yes, this is extremely hard for us to do because our flesh wants to hold off for revenge, or our flesh feels that if we forgive then that means we are saying that what the person did was okay. It isn't. You might want to read Appendix B where the forgiveness process is discussed in more detail.

I bring up forgiveness because this is something within our control and its outcome has tremendous impact on helping us control our emotional states.

A lot of people feel they have no control over their emotions. They believe emotions are what they are and we can't change them or control them. This is not true. To get an accurate view of how emotions come into play, let's look at the following flow chart.

Beliefs... cause

Thoughts ... cause

Emotions ... cause

Struggles to make the right decision ... cause

Decisions ... cause

Actions ... cause

Outcomes ... cause

Habits ... cause

Our character

You will notice that emotions do not cause our thoughts, but it's the other way around. We will get further into this in the next chapter on Challenge My Beliefs. But for right now I want you to see that there are processes that occur before our emotions develop; therefore, we do have the capacity to change the process for a different emotional outcome.

Tapping Away Overwhelm

There is also a physical element that is not listed in the above process that most people are unaware of it. Once we understand that everything is made up of energy, including our thoughts, then we can see how some of our memories could interfere with the free flow of the energy within our bodies. Thus keeping us stuck in our negative emotional state.

The theory is that *the cause of all negative emotions is a disruption in the body's energy system.* It's like your negative emotion gets stuck inside one or more of these energy meridian pathways and stays there until it is relieved by physically using Tapping. So no matter how much counseling you have, or how many self-help books you read, or whatever else you do to try to get rid of your negative emotions, they remain in your meridian energy pathways until physically dealt with.

This is great news because once you use Tapping, you can have very quick results. In fact, you do not have to replay in your mind every detail of what caused that negative emotion in the first place. Your current negative emotion is not caused by your "memory" of that event. Your energy flow in your body got disrupted at the time of the event (or the continual rehashing of that event with emotions). Therefore, we do not need to go into great detail of your memories. This means that doing Tapping does not bring on more negative emotional feelings.

Yes, you will be asked to briefly recall your problem, which may bring on some discomfort, but that is all. Then we apply Tapping to that event and release the emotion that is stuck in our meridian pathways.

Through Tapping we deal with the physical and psychological causes of the disruption in our energy flow, not the resulting negative emotion. Think of it this way:

Distressing Event ... causes

Disruption in the Body's Energy System ... causes

Negative Emotions

Most counseling methods try to treat the memory behind the negative emotion, but fail to deal with the physical disruption in the body's energy system.

This disruption in the body's energy system causes all kinds of problems. They include guilt, anger, fears, phobias, anger, grief, anxiety, depression, traumatic memories, P.T.S.D., worry, guilt, and all our limiting emotions that hold us back from becoming who we want to be or doing what we know we should be doing.

The medical profession has long known that negative emotional issues affect our body's chemistry and, in turn, can lead to everything from rashes and headaches, to impaired immune systems, cancers, etc. And positive emotions can lead to healing of physical ailments!

Because a lot of physical problems are caused by our negative emotions, once we deal with the underlying causes (both mental and physical), our physical problems go away.

Tapping is an emotional version of acupuncture, except it doesn't use needles. It uses a two-prong approach wherein you (1) mentally "tune in" to a specific issue while (2) stimulating certain meridian points on your body by tapping on them with your fingertips. A meridian is any of the pathways in your body along which vital energy flows.

At this point I suggest you review Appendix A which sets forth the Tapping process, including the locations of the energy meridians in our bodies. Examples of Tapping sequences are provided in the appendix for quick use by you. Let's move on to review the emotional states to Tap upon.

Current Negative Emotions

In chapter 2 we listed a variety of negative emotions we may be experiencing. I want to reiterate a few of the major ones here.

- Overwhelming grief
- Anger
- Hopelessness
- Depression
- Anxiety
- Blaming others
- Regret you couldn't help your loved one who passed away
- Helpless over many situations
- Sadness
- Fear of what might happen next

Each of these emotions is listed in Appendix A with examples of Tapping sequences to get you started to overcome each. If there is a particular emotion or situation that is dominating you right now, you may want to begin Tapping on it immediately.

Remember that Tapping is used not only to relieve negative emotions, but also to instill new positive emotions, even if you don't know how that new emotion will play out in your life at the moment.

New Emotions to Inspire You

As you go through the following list of possible new emotions to inspire you, find a situation you want to attach that emotion to. For instance, if you want hope, what are you hoping for? If it is a feeling of control, over what area(s) in your life or particular situation do you want to feel more in control of?

- Hope
- Feelings of being in control
- Expect miracles

- Confidence to handle whatever comes your way
- A deeper loving relationship with your spouse (chapter 7 discusses this further)
- Excitement for the new vision for my future
- I am an overcomer!
- Motivation / Enthusiasm
- Optimism
- Serenity – acceptance of myself and the situations

Be sure to review this chapter and write your thoughts in your journal on the emotions that touch you, negative or positive.

Knowledge, Skills & Habits Needed

This area of controlling our emotions is not a one-time solving of our problems. This process continues throughout the rest of our lives. Therefore, keeping this information in the forefront of your mind every day keeps things from becoming overwhelming, depressing, and hopeless. This is why Tapping is listed as one of the Daily Rituals discussed in chapter 11. Here are the skills and habits necessary to conquer this ongoing battle.

- Tapping away the negative emotions
- Tapping to instill positive changes
- Journaling
- Completing your Daily Rituals (see chapter 11 and Appendix D)

Although you are the one reading this book, these principles can also be taught to your children.

* * * * * * *

During the moments when we are feeling overwhelmed by our emotions we try our best to control them, with little result. No matter how much we try to divert our attention, sometimes we just can't escape our emotions. That's because they do have a physical hold on us. And to break that physical hold requires we do something physical. The skill used to break this physical hold is Tapping.

The day I learned that my friend was going to go into hospice, I fell apart emotionally, and tried to contain my emotions all day—but couldn't. They overwhelmed me. I was easily triggered to start crying at any moment. When I remembered how Tapping helped me in the past, I knew I had to try it on this emotional overwhelm. Like I said earlier, I don't always remember to do Tapping, but when I do, I am always astonished at the quick results.

As I sat on the side of my bed after a very long day and tried to calm myself before going to sleep, I began Tapping. I like to say out loud the phrases. My problem is that I can't cry and talk at the same time. But I forced myself to say the words, and pause if I needed so I could allow the crying. I did several rounds of Tapping on my grief over how much I was going to miss being around her, seeing her infectious smile, listening to her humor, and hearing her words of wisdom. When I felt myself being calm again, I sat there in amazement of how quickly I calmed down. It is such a great feeling to know I have a skill that can give me this tremendous emotional relief in such a short period of time. And that is why I wrote this book—to provide you with the skills to reach a level of peace, calmness, and hope for a brighter future.

Even as I type this, I well up in tears thinking about my friend, but it is not overwhelming, And that's okay! It's okay to grieve and cry over the loss of a loved one. However, when the grief takes over all of our thoughts and spirals into self-pity and overwhelm, that is when we need to do Tapping to keep ourselves on a steady course of going forward in life, not backwards.

Whether you believe that Tapping can provide this fast of a change in you, is based upon your current beliefs—which may need to be challenged. Let's look at how we can challenge and change our current beliefs.

Chapter 5

Challenge My Beliefs

> *Times of chaos lead us into positive or negative growth, there is no in-between.*
> ~Kathy Williamson

During this COVID-19 pandemic a lot of our beliefs are being challenged. And who or what we choose to believe reveals our patterns of beliefs that influence our thinking. Today's news and social media posts come from naysayers, doomsday talkers, conspiracy promoters, medical doctors, politicians, world organizations, local authorities, and the list goes on. How does this affect our emotions?

Our emotions arise from our personal interpretation of events and what people say. Our interpretation is based upon our underlying beliefs, whether we are aware of them or not. Growing into adulthood we began to question what our parents and society taught us to believe. We established our own set of beliefs, yet still aware of our old beliefs. With the rise of a worldwide pandemic and its personal effects on our lives, our minds begin to question things again. This time of chaos leads us into positive or negative growth, there is no in-between. Things are changing and trying to stay neutral leads to a state of confusion, overwhelm, and a life going in a downward spiral.

If we want a different outcome, we've got to change our thinking and the words we speak. Once we change our beliefs, then the correct thoughts and words follow. How do we know what our current beliefs are? Look at the outcomes in our lives. What are the thoughts we rehearse over and over? What words do we speak out loud? Do we speak fear or optimism? Some people ask:

"How can we speak optimism when our society is falling apart? I have no job, the place I worked at is now permanently closed. My unemployment isn't enough to cover everything. I'm behind in my rent. I live in fear of being evicted and becoming homeless. My children are getting on my nerves from not being able to go play with their friends. I can't even get a hug from my friends who have always supported me. I have a relative who has the virus and we all live in fear of him dying. And we haven't recovered from the death of our father from COVID-19. We weren't even given an opportunity to tell him goodbye and that we loved him. We can't attend church where we enjoyed being around our Christian friends and being in the presence of God. And you want me to be optimistic about my future!"

I understand there are no quick fixes to these situations. However, the emotional overwhelm from living under these circumstances can be brought down to a level which allows you to function in a manner to see possibilities for a new life beyond COVID-19. I am not advocating that we forget what has happened to us during this pandemic, nor that we don't have a right to be upset. A lot of these experiences will change our lives forever.

The goals of this book are to reduce your emotional

overwhelm, give you ideas for building a better life, and provide hope that it is possible to reach your goals in spite of the odds stacked against you. Henry Ford said it best, "Whether you think you can or you think you can't – you're right." The ability to implement the things taught in this book depends upon your choice, attitude, and willingness to try new things in order to grab hold of a better life. Yes, it is possible!

Change Begins In our Mind

Everything we do comes from our beliefs. Our conscious mind (thoughts) deals with our intellect, viewing things from our five senses, making judgments and decisions according to what we see (and not what we believe). Our subconscious mind (our beliefs) controls our embedded behavior. To change our behavior, we need to go through a process that identifies these false beliefs within our subconscious and replace them with truths.

To change our behavior does not come from willpower nor intellectually forcing ourselves to stop certain behavior. It comes from working with our conscious to change and modify what our subconscious does automatically.

How is this done? Whatever picture is visualized in our minds, with the emotion of it already manifesting, is what the subconscious goes to work on to make it happen externally. It used to bother me that people would say that your mind understands every word except the word "no." Then I learned that our mind operates off of pictures, not words. The picture in your mind always overrides your thoughts or words. That is why when a person says, "I don't want to be broke any more," the picture and the emotions of being broke are flashed across their mind. Subsequently, that is what materializes in their outer world. Our mind operates from pictures, and our words (and thoughts) create that picture. Change our thoughts and the pictures they produce, and we can change our lives!

I coach a lot of people who are stuck in their problems. Here are some of the statements I repeatedly hear that hold people back from moving on in their life.

- I can't handle this.
- I don't know what to do.
- I can't do that!
- I can't motivate myself to do anything.
- I'll never forgive that person.
- I'm mentally disabled and can't do that. (May be partially true.)
- I'm not worthy of living a better life.
- It's hopeless. I've been trying for years to change my life and I just can't.
- I can't forgive myself.
- I'll never get ahead financially.
- I'll never lose this weight.

To uncover limiting beliefs, add the word "because" at the end of your current belief and then finish the sentence. Example: "I can't handle this because: it's too hard ... too emotional ... I've tried in the past and failed ... it stirs up too many negative emotions ... I'm too old to change ... I will disappoint my parents (or spouse, friend, etc.). " Take a moment and identify the above thoughts that you may be having, and then complete the sentence using 'because.' What beliefs showed up for you? I encourage you to write these down so you know what beliefs need to be questioned.

Current Beliefs / Self-Talk

Let's take a look at some current thoughts and/or verbal statements that may be holding us back during this time of pandemic:

- I can't change until I know what the new society will look like once the pandemic is under control or gone.

- All my dreams for my career are down the drain and I just can't start over.
- I don't have control over what my future will look like.
- I'm not sure I have the desire, stamina or ability to start over.
- I'm disgusted and angry that so many people have turned this pandemic into a heated political arena.
- Nobody cares about me or the sorrow I'm going through after my loved one passed away.
- My constitutional rights have been taken away from me and I can't do anything about it.
- I'm going to show 'them' that they can't mess with me!

Once again, to determine your underlying beliefs, add the word 'because' to the statements you hear yourself thinking or speaking and finish the sentence.

How do we know if what we believe is true or a lie? Do we have a foundational set of rights and wrongs that we weigh our beliefs against? What do you use as your standard? Most people base their beliefs and actions upon what they were taught while growing up. As children, we never questioned them because we thought that our parents would not teach us anything that would harm us. Yet, as we grew into adulthood and began to see different points of views, we saw we had a choice to believe differently. With a broader influx of views from people and society, we began to form our own identity based upon new input. Is it time to once again question what we believe?

I was raised going to church every Sunday. My parents were very strict and conservative. I grew up with some pretty dogmatic beliefs. Once I was an adult I had the freedom to identify and change these beliefs. I became a Christian in 1980 and I use the standards set forth in the Bible to form my beliefs. This is a life-long process of changing our beliefs. I am in my 60s and still work hard to change some of the underlying beliefs that hold me back. So don't think this is a one-time change.

Our beliefs in our subconscious mind are so intertwined with each other and so vast, where do we begin to change? The bigger the contrast between what we currently believe and the truth we discover, the longer it takes to process it in our mind and to make the choice to believe what is true. However, using Tapping will greatly reduce the time it takes to change our beliefs. It helps to see how our beliefs and our thinking affect everything we do. Once again, the following sets forth the correct order of our thought process:

> Beliefs ... result in
>
> Thoughts ... result in
>
> Emotions ... result in
>
> Struggle to make the right decision ... result in
>
> Decisions ... result in
>
> Actions ... result in
>
> Habits ... result in
>
> Character ... result in
>
> Destiny!

It is important to understand that some people believe that circumstances, experiences or emotions cause our thoughts. But our thoughts are based upon what we believe about those circumstances or experiences or our perception of them. Our emotions come as a result of what we think about—the picture we have in our mind. Sometimes we need to backtrack into this process to find out what is going on. If you do something and you're not sure why you're doing it, ask yourself the following questions:

What emotions triggered my actions?

What thoughts triggered my emotions?

What beliefs (or perceptions) triggered my thoughts?

Are those beliefs true or false?

I suggest you write down what you have discovered in your thought life. What thoughts keep showing up that hold you back from moving forward in life? What are the self-talk statements that you find yourself rehashing over and over? If you identify the underlying beliefs to your thoughts, and you whole-heartedly believe they are true—will you be open to the possibility that they may not be true? Growth requires us to be willing to learn new things and embrace new perspectives.

If we find ourselves always talking about our past hurts, we must be honest with ourselves and ask whether we do it to get sympathy from others for what we went through. I did this a lot, because I didn't know how to get love and attention in a healthy manner. I didn't know how to receive love. By going through the process in this book I believe you will be able to make the shift from looking for love and attention through doing negative things, to receiving love and attention as a by-product of your new lifestyle.

New Empowering Beliefs / Self-Talk

Let's take a look at how to instill empowering beliefs and self-talk to overcome any emotional overwhelm we may be going through. Using the negative emotions listed in chapter 4, below is a comparison to show you some examples.

Overwhelming Grief

Old: This grief is too much. I can't handle it.

New: I can handle this grief and not let it overwhelm me.

Anger

Old: I can't stop being angry.

New: I can release my anger, forgive people, and choose to change my focus.

Hopelessness

Old: There is absolutely no hope of my life getting better.

New: I choose to create a better life for myself and rise above my circumstances.

Depression

Old: I'm depressed and I can't do anything about it.

New: My depression is caused by what I think about. I choose to dwell on the awesome future I have planned out.

Anxiety

Old: I have no control over these anxiety attacks.

New: Because I am now focused on the bright future I have planned for myself, my anxiety is gone as a by-product of that new focus.

Blaming Others

Old: My negative outlook on life is caused by the negative circumstances forced upon me by my family and friends, politicians, governmental rules, and by society. I did not choose to be controlled by them.

New: Although I now need to live under certain restrictions until COVID-19 is under control and life reopens for everyone, I take full responsibility for my reactions and choose to not let these things pull me down. This is only a temporary situation.

Regret Over Loved One Passing Away

Old: I feel regret that I couldn't be with my loved one before his or her death.

New: I release my feelings of regret because I did everything I could under the circumstances to try to be with my loved one. My loved one is out of pain and is now in heaven living a great life. My loved one would not want me to continue being angry and regretful over their death. My loved one would want me to move on with my life and live it fully.

Helpless Over Many Situations

Old: My hands are tied, I can't do what I want to do to help others. I feel helpless to be able to improve things.

New: I may not be able to do what I used to do to help others, but I can still pray for those people and provide encouragement as often as I can.

Sadness

Old: I am overwhelmed with sadness and feel stuck.

New: Yes, the current state of affairs in my life and the world make me sad. However, I choose to look at the bright future that will emerge from this trial.

Fear of What Might Happen Next

Old: With all the negative things going on in my life, I'm waiting for the next shoe to fall.

New: Yes, parts of my future life cannot be predicted at the moment. I choose to believe that I will come out of this a better person with better circumstances.

Now I want you to write out your current beliefs/self-talk, and then write out your new belief and the self-talk to support it.

Knowledge, Skills & Habits Needed

Several things help us to change our beliefs, thoughts and resulting actions. One is the vision we create for our awesome future. This gives us something to turn our thoughts toward. As we build our mental picture of the future we desire, we have something to excite us and give us the emotional fuel we need to keep headed in the right direction.

One aspect of using Tapping is that when we do tapping, our minds may tend to get sidetracked onto other thoughts related to what we are tapping on. Those side trails reveal areas we need to tap on also. Remember, there is no right or wrong wording to use while tapping. If your mind wanders to other areas, then that is a prominent issue in your life that should be dealt with.

Tapping regarding our beliefs helps us tremendously. As we uncover what might be our underlying false beliefs, we can tap on the release of our attachment to them and tap about our willingness to be open to new beliefs, if in fact they are false. As you tap you may also find that the more you tap, the stronger your conviction gets that the idea is the truth.

Many people think they have to know what their underlying emotional blockages are before they can be cleared or released. However, tapping assists us to overcome them, just by tapping for clarity on why we can't do what we want to do.

As indicated earlier, forgiveness brings freedom to our lives. What about our beliefs around whether we can or cannot forgive that person right away? Or the belief that it is wrong if I don't get upset at what's happening in our society? What about our belief that *if only I had been with my loved one, he or she wouldn't have died because my presence would have been the motivation for that person to fight to live*?

* * * * * * *

I have been thinking a lot lately about an interesting concept. So many people, myself included, believe(d) that we have emotional blockages that are keeping us from moving forward and doing what we want to do in life. But is that really true? How would I know when that blockage is gone? Would I feel differently? Not sure. Would I act differently? Definitely, and that is how I would know.

Therefore, my focus on the fact that I have emotional blockages may not be true. But because I keep telling myself I have these blockages that I can't seem to identify, is that what's keeping me stuck? This self-talk? What if I tell myself that I don't have any emotional blockages, that I can do what I want, and discover the steps to carry out what I desire to do? My focus would then be on taking action for a great future, and not focused on my old ways of thinking that I can't. Something to think about!

I have been beating myself up mentally for years, telling myself I have some sort of emotional blockages (which I could never identify). Then an "ah ha" moment occurred when I learned at a conference held by Brendon Burchard that my failures were not because of "who I am," but because I was not using the right practices and habits that will change me. My lack of knowledge about this held me back, and I kept thinking it was *me* when it really wasn't. This applies to all areas of our lives.

Repetition is a big factor in being able to change our beliefs. Repetition of what we want to believe, repetition of the new practices and principles I am learning, repetition of seeing myself carrying out these practices and visualizing new results in my life. Repetition requires us to be intentional in our daily living. That's why I created the Daily Rituals set out in chapter 11.

Part of being able to change our beliefs is to be able to identify any underlying issues we can't recognize unless we intentionally look for them. The next chapter tells us how to do that.

Chapter 6

Clarify Underlying Issues

> *Permanent change won't come until underlying issues are identified and resolved.* ~Kathy Williamson

Hopefully we have already uncovered a lot of underlying issues so far. This chapter discusses that if we are not aware of underlying issues that cause our emotional behaviors, and address those issues, then those issues keep triggering us and we keep running in circles our whole life. Even though you may feel you don't have any underlying issues, I suggest you read this chapter to gain knowledge that will allow you to help friends and loved ones who may be avoiding their underlying issues. You may be surprised what might show up in your own life as you read this chapter.

This particular step I use mostly when I am coaching people stuck in their addiction or alcoholism. I personally do not believe in the disease model for addictions, but rather believe there are underling issues that cause a person to escape the negative feelings arising from those issues by utilizing their addiction. Once the underlying issue(s) are identified and resolved, then the addict will no longer be triggered. However, there is more to this process to change the life of an addict or their loved ones. The addict must follow all steps in the Roadmap to Freedom in order to stop relapsing forever.

My heart also goes out to the loved ones of addicts. I was an addict for 10 years, and I was also married to an ex-addict, narcissistic, and pathological liar who sucked the life out of me. But I was able to take back my life. From this unique perspective of having lived in the shoes of both sides of this relationship, I wrote a book *My Friend Is An Addict – What Can I Do? Use the Roadmap Out of Addiction to Influence the Addict and to Take Back Your Life* (for sale on Amazon). The book was written to provide the loved ones of addicts with specific steps to take back control of their life, and use the same process to influence the addict. The Roadmap set forth in that book is not identified as cleanly as my *Roadmaps To Freedom: Personal Growth Transformation That Sticks* set forth in this book.

Current Underlying Issues

A lot of our underlying issues regarding our overwhelming negative emotions come in the form of:

- Lack of knowledge
- False beliefs
- Being unaware we have once again fallen back into our old thoughts and behaviors
- Not putting words to the emotions we are feeling, thus leaving us confused
- Having too many things on our plate to do
- Lack of vision for a brighter future
- Any unresolved issues from our past (childhood, trauma, health issues, etc.) have been pushed down even further as we focus on our current state of survival.

- Anger, but we don't know what is causing it
- A focus on determining how to survive an unknown future, and losing out on living our life to its fullest today.
- Letting the winds of change blow us through life to a place we don't want to be, instead of learning to maneuver the winds to our advantage so we can reach our goals in life.

We may have had a lot of these underlying issues before the COVID-19 pandemic began. The onslaught of more negative emotions that got pent up inside us brought us to a point we have never been at in our lives.

Sometimes awareness alone of these issues will help us resolve them. However, we are creatures of habit and without some form of daily reminders on what to stay focused on, we easily slip back into our old patterns. Therefore, in chapter 11 I set forth some "Daily Rituals For a New You." This set of morning and evening rituals will give you a starting point on staying focused on the things that will draw you into a brighter future. They are also listed in Appendix D for quick reference.

Have you identified your underlying issues? If so, write them down so you can have a clear picture of things you need to work on. Writing things down helps to put clarity to the thoughts mulling around in our minds. Once written, we can prioritize which areas to work on first. This is how to overcome the feelings of overwhelm we get by having too much on our plate.

Not all issues can be resolved through this book, but a majority of them can. If you are willing to apply the knowledge you learn and develop new skills and habits.

Knowledge, Skills & Habits Needed

To clarify any underlying issues, a lot has already been

discussed to help you sort out what's going on in your life. Knowledge is a big factor in identifying and overcoming these issues. Sometimes we can't see the big picture because we are so focused on the minute parts of it.

Skills & Habits needed:

Tapping – when you tap on what you do know is an issue, sometimes your mind will stray into other things that are related. If this happens, then tap on those issues to resolve them. The good thing about Tapping is that we don't need to always know what our underlying issue is. We can tap on the thought or behavior we want to change, which may have resulted from an underlying issue, and the Tapping will clear it out of our system. We don't have to "relive" our past in order for it to get resolved.

Forgiveness – please be willing to forgive that person today. Also be willing to forgive yourself for things you have or have not done in your life. Remember from reading about forgiveness in Appendix B that part of the process is to stop rehashing the hurt from that incident. It is over. Yesterday is over and we cannot change it. We can learn from it and move on. Choose today to switch your focus from the hurt that people or circumstances have caused you—to focusing on your vision for your bright future. But don't forget to live today to its fullest!

Daily Rituals – I mention this here, even though it is not covered until chapter 11, so you can add this to your arsenal to help you beat the odds stacked against you! It will help you to develop new habits in each of these areas.

One of the daily rituals is in the evening to review how well we handled our emotions that day. The sooner we can catch our negative focus, the sooner we can reduce our emotional overwhelm. Knowledge alone does not help us. We heed to apply the knowledge and we do that by actions. These daily rituals help us stay on track every day. Without them, we start heading down the slippery road to emotional overwhelm.

* * * * * * *

I want to share with you at this point a personal story which shows you the application of the principles taught so far. You will notice that even though I created this process and teach it to others, life still happens and I have to reapply what I know to my life too.

As I was writing this chapter I went through another period of total negativity which soon became overwhelming. One night I couldn't fall asleep because I was so upset about a couple of people and how they were negatively affecting my life. So as I lay there I stewed and stewed and finally told myself things had to change.

I realized I was in the same negative mindset that I teach others how to overcome—so I needed to apply the process to my situation. I had to go back to the first step *Choose Your Destination* and recognize that I was totally focused only on this situation and rehashing in my thoughts and words all the negative aspects of it. It was time for me to make better choices on how to handle my reactions, which were causing my emotional turmoil, not the two ladies.

The first step was for me to figure out where I wanted to go—instead of staying focused on the fact that I wanted to get out of my circumstances, but I did not see a way out. So I had to bring myself back to the vision I have for my future. I have a vision/prayer board with pictures representing where I want to go (it contains my top 3 business goals and top 3 personal goals for the next year). So I spent some time focusing on and praying over that vision.

Then I had to figure out what would get me out of my current negative situation, until more things opened up for me to pursue my vision. I tend to see things in black and white. This meant I thought I needed to totally change *all* the circumstances in order to resolve the problem. In reality, there was one solution that would allow me to remove these two ladies' negative impact on my life, rather than having to change my entire outward circumstances. I came up with a solution—to forgive, forget and move on—and then kept that at the center of my attention.

The next step was to ask myself *who do I need to forgive?* and *who do I need to ask forgiveness from?* There were two ladies involved in these unrelated situations. One I had to forgive. The other I had to ask for her forgiveness. The first lady I forgave in my heart at that moment. The next morning I sent a text to the other lady whom I needed to apologize to, and got relief from that part of my negative situation. What a dramatic difference in my emotional state in less than 24 hours!

What were some of my underlying issues?

- The habit of looking only at the negative and continually rehash it in my mind and build my emotions into a frenzy. Then tell others about it to get their sympathy. (Ouch! That's hard to admit!)
- I fell back into my negative thoughts that brought up similar situations from my past to validate my current response to the situation.
- The pictures in my mind were all about this situation. Therefore, the situation continued to grow worse.
- Not recognizing this pattern of thought earlier than I did.

As you can see, the process of reducing our emotional overwhelm can be applied quickly with great results. But how could I keep myself from getting in this situation in the first place? In chapter 11 you will discover Daily Rituals to carry out every morning and evening. My first goal is in the evening to review my emotional state from that day. Did I focus only on the negative? Or did I stop my negative thinking and switch to focusing on the awesome future I want to build? The ideal is to catch myself as early as possible of this negative focus, stop it, and change focus immediately. If I feel I just can't control my thoughts, then I verbalize my dreams for my future. And sure enough, the negative thoughts and anxieties reside.

I hope you can see how this material can be applied to our lives. On your list of underlying issues, spend some time by yourself thinking about how to resolve them and shift your focus.

In the next chapter we look at how to communicate with purpose and the purpose is not always self-centered.

Chapter 7

Communicate With Purpose

> *Love never fails. 1 Cor. 13:8 (NIV)*

Do we ever stop and think about how we communicate with others? Do we just spurt out whatever comes to mind, without checking first to determine if what we are about to say will hurt or help the situation? Is there a purpose of communication beyond our selfish desires? Are we speaking things just because we know that's what the other person wants to hear? Or are we speaking things to intentionally hurt someone? Do others view us as being harsh or brash in the way we interact with them? Do we let our feelings control what comes out of our mouths? Are we known as a lover or as a fighter?

Before this pandemic, we knew that if we were forced to stay indoors for too long, we become irritable, short-tempered, and we get on each other's nerves. But we knew that our time of isolation would end at the close of our vacation or whatever caused our having to be indoors. Not so today. COVID-19 brought on a whole new dynamic of what isolation is and our resulting behaviors. At this point in time, we are still unsure of what our future holds in terms of how soon we will be allowed in social gatherings without "social distancing" or having to wear masks. This fear of the unknown has added to our emotional overwhelm.

Being in isolation has highlighted our flaws in our communication habits. For many, the worse of who we are has surfaced. It has turned into major depression for many, especially the elderly who only had one or two friends to interact with. Talking with someone over the phone or texting is not the same as being in their physical presence. No hugs. No smiles. No touch of a hand on the shoulder to encourage. No crying together over the loss of a loved one. No seeing the face of excitement over the future. No sharing of personal vibes to help one through a tough time. The downward spiral of our outlook on life can get out of control very fast. It sucks!

Communication skills apply to the words we speak, write, and our self-talk. Our body language also speaks loudly. But I want to stay focused on becoming aware of our style of communicating and learning new ways that will greatly improve our relationships with others and ourselves.

Is there one primary goal in life that mankind can seek where the positive effects of it trickle down into all areas of our lives? As a Christian my main focus is to do what Jesus has told me to do:

"Love the Lord your God with all your heart and with all your soul and with all your mind." This is the first and greatest commandment. And the second is like it: "Love your neighbor as yourself." Matthew 22:37-39 (NIV)

Why is this perspective so important? Because according to 1 Corinthians 13:8, *Love never fails*. What does this mean? If we put love as our top priority in everything we do, especially our communication, the love brings results we never could have dreamed. This can be difficult when we are dealing with a person we really want to hate. Once again, I must turn to how Jesus has instructed me to treat those I want to hate:

"You have heard that it was said, 'Love your neighbor and hate your enemy.' But I tell you, love your enemies and pray for those who persecute you ..." Matthew 5:43-44 (NIV)

This requires a life-long commitment, and I do admit it is not always easy to do. Yes, there are some people who we need to avoid being around, but if we are stuck in a situation (work, family member, etc.) then this principle should guide us.

One more aspect of what love can do—is it can make our fears disappear. The Bible states in 1 John 4:18 (NIV): *There is no fear in love. But perfect love drives out fear, because fear has to do with punishment. The one who fears is not made perfect in love* . Therefore, we must bring love into every interaction with people, as well as in our self-talk.

Bring Love Into Every Situation

Every person seeks love and significance in life. Love takes on a life of its own and can do things we can't do. It fills the deepest hole in our soul. Most people do not understand that, according to the Bible, when love is brought into a situation, it never fails. What does that mean? One meaning is that God's love toward us never fails nor never ends. God's love is unconditional and will never be withdrawn from us. Another viewpoint is that although we may not feel love toward a person, we can allow God's love to flow through us to that person and make its impact.

What does this have to do with bringing love into every situation when human love can be finicky? Even though our love is not pure like God's love, we sometimes make it conditional or hold back until we feel it is okay to love that person. But if we make a decision to show love no matter what, it takes on a magical presence and does things beyond what we are trying to accomplish. However, how do we exactly show love to people?

Know The 5 Love Languages

As different personalities exist, so do different ways to express love. Understanding these differences will transform every relationship you're in. Once you know your love language, then you can share it with others so they will know how to show their love toward you in a manner that you will know it is love.

You also need to determine what the love language is for each of the people with whom you interact on a regular basis. This can be done by observing the person, or by asking them. They may not know at first, but after reading the following material you can help them to identify their own love language.

I suggest you read the book *The 5 Love Languages: The Secret To Love That Lasts* by Gary Chapman. Also, *The 5 Love Languages of Teens: The Secret To Loving Teens Effectively* by Gary Chapman. Basically, five types of love languages exist; and within each type there exists a variety of ways to express that type of love. Let's take a brief look at each of them.

Words of Affirmation – Do you crave compliments, words of encouragement, or words of kindness spoken to you in a humble manner? While most people need words of affirmation, some can get along fine with only a word or two now and then. But if you only recognize someone's love towards you based upon how often they complement you or give you words of encouragement, then this type of love may be your main theme.

Quality Time – The type of time focused on within this language is togetherness time. This is where you give each other focused attention with quality conversation. You share experiences, thoughts, feelings and desires. It's seen as a time to build a relationship, not to work on a project or on a problem to be solved. Rather than seeking advice, you are seeking understanding. It's a time of sympathetic listening with a view to understanding the other person's thoughts, feelings and desires. Together you learn how to reveal yourselves to each other. This quality time can include quality activities.

Receiving Gifts – What person doesn't like to receive gifts? So you have to compare the other types of love languages to see whether this style of love is your main way of feeling loved. Gifts include both tangible and intangible things. Being physically present with someone during a crisis is powerful in this category.

Acts of Service – You tend to do things for others or you expect to receive acts of service from others. It's important for you and the other person to know what the *specific type of service* is that you recognize as love being shown toward you. Your spouse may do a lot of acts of service, but if they're not the ones that you consider important, it doesn't count—and he or she won't know that unless you tell them.

Physical Touch – Some people are natural "touchers" while others can't stand to be touched. This can cause a lot of problems if one desires to be touched and never gets touched (hugs, hand on the shoulder, hold hands, etc.). This is an area where you usually have to let your spouse know that you enjoy being touched and that it is a way you recognize that he/she loves you. If you don't tell your spouse, they will never know and you will continue to feel unloved. Most women deeply desire to be held whenever they cry and receive extra hugs during a time of crisis.

While the above is a brief description of each type of love language, it helps to understand that we usually show love to others in the same manner that we want it shown to us. So if you see yourself already demonstrating love to someone else through one of the above situations, look inside yourself to see if that is how you also want to be shown love. But recognize that this may not be that person's love language.

Many times children grow up thinking they are unloved. In reality, they needed to be shown love in one manner, but their parents showed love in their own way, which did not signal love to the child. Looking back on your childhood, do you recognize this? I sure do! In fact, I grew up telling others that I was raised in a home without love or communication. It wasn't until well into my adulthood that I recognized that my parents did love me, but they showed their love in a manner that was outside of my love language; therefore, I did not recognize it as love.

Understanding these love languages is vital to help you learn how to develop healthy, loving relationships.

Another eye opener is to determine your child's love language, especially if you're having trouble with your teenager. Don't be afraid to ask them. They may not know, so going over the five types and discussing what each style looks like will help them recognize their love language.

Current Communication Style

Let's take a look at how our communication may have gotten off track during the pandemic. Here are some examples of thinking (and self-talk) and communication that we may find ourselves stuck in:

- Self-pity
- Blaming others (people close to you or governments)
- Rehashing all the negative things that have happened to us

- We keep thinking and verbalizing a bleak future
- Nobody understands what we are going through
- Expressing our hopelessness over and over
- Discussing world events, leading to additional fear and anxiety
- Telling ourselves "I can't handle this," "I don't know what to do [to change my life]," "That won't work in my life," "If you didn't do (this) then I wouldn't be feeling the way I am," "I can't change careers at my age," "There was never enough money, and now I don't even have that amount coming in," "If the kids would just obey me, then I wouldn't feel so overwhelmed," etc.
- If you lost a loved one, these may be some things you keep repeating, "I can't handle this grief on top of everything else I'm going through," "If I could have seen that the person was sick sooner, then perhaps death could have been avoided," "I feel bad because I couldn't tell that person how much I loved them," "If I could have been by her/his side to be an advocate and fight for her/him, I might have been able to save them," "I feel bad that she/he had to be alone at their time of death," etc.

You can probably add your own list of internal thoughts you think and/or express over a variety of situations.

I am not trying to draw you away from the realities of what you are going through, but I am trying to help you to be open to seeing alternative thinking and ways to communicate (to yourself and to others).

I suggest you grab pen and paper and sit by yourself for a while. Write down the thoughts you find yourself rehashing. What are the circumstances or beliefs you believe are causing you to think this way? Do you believe you can think differently despite your circumstances? Why or why not? You can add the word "because" at the end of your statement and the way you complete your sentence helps you identify your underlying beliefs.

Throughout our lives we are conditioned to think and respond to situations in a specific way. We tend to blame people or circumstances for how things are going in our lives. But what if that is a false premise? What if we can *choose* to respond differently? Instead of knee-jerk reactions, both mentally and physically, let's choose to take 100% responsibility for our lives from today forward. This means we decide how we want to live. We decide to live from a position of love, hope, and to walk in faith that a better future awaits us. This is what it will take to plan out a new future for ourselves.

Communication is the key element to begin this change. Yes, we will need to examine and change some of our underlying beliefs. Those beliefs show up in our thought life and the words we speak. Therefore, it's vital we learn to control them, change them, and through repetition our lives get changed. Let's look at where we want to go in our new, empowered, and intentional communication.

New Purposeful Communication

Hopefully you have identified some of the thoughts or ways of communication you wish to change. In light of overcoming emotional overwhelm, here are some new ways to do so.

- If you lost a loved one during this pandemic, share with family and friends positive memories of your loved one (not the terrible circumstances surrounding their death).
- You can create a Memory Book about the loved one you lost and purposely seek out contributions from others. Fill your book with pictures and ask others to provide a letter highlighting that person's life, even if it is only one or two sentences.

- If you find yourself having knee-jerk reactions to people's comments, determine why it causes such a quick response, and determine ahead of time a better way to respond (communicate).
- Do you have friends who entice you to do the wrong things and you easily get sucked into doing them? Determine ahead of time a better way to respond to keep yourself from going down that slippery road to destruction.
- Communicate with your family and friends about the 5 Love Languages you just learned about and have a great ongoing discussion about them.
- Focus on listening to others more than talking about your own hurts.
- Share your vision for your awesome future. Help someone close to you develop an awesome vision for their life too. Buy them a copy of this book for their own use.
- Apologize to others if necessary. Ask for forgiveness from them if needed. Saying "I'm sorry" is not enough. Perhaps say, "I'm sorry for what I said, will you forgive me?" And then stop rehashing the event.
- Ask the people close to you for their input on how your relationships could get stronger and have more meaning.
- Ask people how you can help them (physically, emotionally, spiritually).
- Your new self-talk will be the most powerful thing you can do. Go back and review some of the new thoughts listed in chapter 5.
- Communication about the new vision for your life is very empowering. However, be careful who you share your vision with as not everyone will be supportive of it. Part of spending 80% of your free time working on building your new vision includes your self-talk about how you can do it and how good it will feel to accomplish that vision.

- If you don't have anyone speaking encouragement into your life, you might search the Internet and YouTube to find people who inspire you through their talks, seminars, books, coaching, etc. It's up to us to be proactive in getting more positive input into our lives. Facebook groups may be another helpful place; however, be careful not to get sidetracked by some people's negative comments. Be diligent in deciding what groups to join.

Communication input you may need to avoid (or limit your contact with):

- If hearing the bad news about how our societies and the world are struggling, then perhaps it is time to take a break from watching or listening to the news.
- Being around negative people will have a tendency to draw you into their realm of doom and gloom.
- People who put you down or damper your dreams.

Grab your pen and paper and write in your journal some new ways for you to communicate and also ways to avoid situations that lead you astray.

Knowledge, Skills & Habits Needed

I suggest you go to Amazon and check out the variety of books Gary Chapman has written to reach various groups of people. I also suggest his *Love Language Minute for Couples: 100 Days to a Closer Relationship*. Check out Appendix E for more resources.

Repetition is the key to instilling new habits, beliefs, thoughts, self-talk, and communication style that permanently change your lifestyle.

****

One experience that was an eye opener for me occurred on one of my jobs as a legal secretary. It was standard procedure to rotate the secretaries among the various bosses in the office. There was one boss who no one wanted to work for, including myself. However, I found myself assigned to this person, despite my protests. After getting over my anger, I decided to put aside my opinions about this person and "just love her." That was my mantra day in and day out.

What did that look like in my actions and words? I would have the self-talk in my head throughout the day of *just love her, everyone needs love, love never fails.* I would intentionally *feel* love toward her to project it to her when I was in her presence. I held back on saying anything that would be seen as negative. I began with small talk about work, a little bit about my personal life, and it eventually led to her talking about her personal life. Over the course of time, not only did my attitude toward her change, but she changed also. At the beginning I would never have believed the outcome that occurred. I have applied this lesson to many situations since then.

Chapter 8

Change My Lifestyle

> *If you stop learning, you stop living.*
> ~Kathy Williamson

Our lifestyle consists of the things we do over and over, most of them unconsciously. In order to change, however, we must be intentional in our words and actions. Let's bring everything together to see the bigger picture of where you are, where you want to go in life, and how to get there. Have your pen and paper ready to answer the questions presented as you review each section covered.

Preparation for the Journey

The three major new skills to learn are: Tapping, forgiveness (and then stop rehashing the event), and create a new vision for your future. Further skills were taught in the chapters that followed.

Have any of these new skills become habits for you? Do you see any significant improvement in any area of your life?

Choose My Destination

Once you identified where you are in your emotional overwhelm, did you also determine the emotional state you wish to pursue? The seven emotional states discussed were: (1) Emotionally—Grief Over situations, (2) Emotionally—Anger/Fears, (3) Physically—Loss of things, (4) Health (COVID Sufferers – Current and Long-Haulers), (5) Financial—Loss of, (6) Relationships—Loss of, and (7) Spiritually—Potential Losses.

What are some of the destinations you chose? You can use Tapping, forgiveness and journaling to help you bring clarity in each of these areas.

Change My Focus

Once again, you need to identify where your current focus is and then how you can change that focus to the new dreams for your life, which brings positive emotions into your life. Did you identify a new, exciting vision for your future? Can you state it in one or two sentences? How can you start implementing it in some manner into your daily or weekly activities to keep you headed in the right direction? If you were to spend 80% of your free time working toward your new vision for your life, what would you be doing? When will you start?

Chapter 3 lists possible emotional states to focus on. Appendix C also mentions putting together a Vision Board of what you want your future to look like. Have you done that?

The skill of journaling allows you to write down specific plans on ways to make your vision become a reality. It allows you to put words to your hopes and dreams for a brighter future. This clarity is needed to help you from falling back into old habits of thinking and talking negative stuff.

Control My Emotions

Did you identify the source(s) that are causing you

emotional overwhelm? Did you use the Tapping technique to reduce the overwhelm? Did it work? Did you give up too early? Did you do it but with a closed mind that it wouldn't work? Are you willing to be open to this marvelous technique that can transform your life?

Did you also use Tapping to instill positive emotions in you? Check out Appendix A for samples of both types of Tapping. Remember, you can also teach your children Tapping. See Appendix E for resources for teaching this technique to children in a manner they can understand it.

Challenge My Beliefs

After reviewing your negative self-talk and looking at the words you have spoken in the last couple of weeks, did you identify some beliefs that may not be true? In chapter 5 I proposed some powerful new beliefs to instill. To change our beliefs requires repetition of new thoughts and words that paint new pictures to support our new beliefs.

What new beliefs did you discover you want to instill into your life? Did you ponder my story about how we may have the problem *only* because we keep telling ourselves we have that problem, instead of taking physical action to do whatever it is we think we can't do?

Write down the new beliefs in such a manner that they resonate with you and get you excited. Then in your Daily Rituals repeat them.

Clarify Underlying Issues

From the list of possible underlying issues in chapter 6 did you identify any of them showing up in your life? Some of the issues may have been present before the pandemic and then got amplified, or pushed away, due to other overwhelming emotions. Tapping on these underlying issues will clear them up. If you end up on a rabbit trail as you Tap on your issues, follow that trail and Tap on it too.

This is an area we need to constantly be aware that we easily fall back into our old beliefs and habits of destruction. Being faithful to do our Daily Rituals will keep us on the right track.

Communicate With Purpose

We can only expect permanent change when we are willing to change our thoughts and words. Did you determine your Love Language? Did you share it with the significant other in your life? Did you help others to determine their Love Language so everyone can help improve their relationships?

Reviewing the list of New Purposeful Communication in chapter 7, which ones are you committed to working on? How can you implement these changes on a daily basis? Are there people you need to remove from having contact with, or limiting your contact with them?

****

The best way I can show you how I put everything together is to share how I used this process to overcome a ten-year addiction to pain medications.

Choose My Destination – Instead of focusing on "not" doing my addiction, I focused on how to make the vision God gave me come to fruition. I became a Christian in 1980 (6 months into my addiction). I began volunteering as a lay counselor on a Christian-based crisis hotline in 1981. In 1984 God showed me that I would someday open my own crisis hotline. But that didn't happen until early 1990—ten long years of being in a state of relapse, even though I was well-grounded in knowing God and Scripture. I never lost sight of my dream to open a hotline.

Change My Focus – I eventually quit going to support groups because I saw it as the blind leading the blind. I had a different set of beliefs. I knew there was a way to get out of the addiction, and it didn't have to take 40 years of attending support groups. When my vision began to come into fruition in early 1990, within three to four months my entire life turned around and I never went back to my addiction!

Control My Emotions – I did not know about Tapping back in the 1980s. I trusted in God's Word that said He will never leave me nor forsake me. The Bible tells me I am capable of controlling my emotions, and therefore able to avoid having to take pain pills to escape from the emotional pain from various things in my life. I now combine my faith in God with Tapping and get quick, permanent relief from emotional overwhelm (and some physical problems too).

Challenge My Beliefs – I never did buy into the theory that addiction is a disease. After I saw many people stuck in support groups for years, I switched my belief away from believing that support groups would help me recover. Life is not meant to be lived centered around a bad habit we once had. I am not an addict, I am a Christian who had a habit of using pain pills to escape my emotional pains. I had to challenge my beliefs that "I" could do what God was asking me to do to open a hotline.

Clarify Underlying Issues – I knew what negative emotions I was trying to escape from. I had to forgive my parents for what I thought was a lack of love toward me while growing up. Then I had to stop rehashing the stories. Yes, I did recognize I was using my past to gain attention and love. However, another issue developed through my years of trying to stop my relapse cycle—I became totally introspective. Life was only about *me, myself, and I*. To overcome this inward focus I used the vision for my future to reach out to love and help others. Remember in the past when you helped someone how much more blessed you felt afterwards? That's the emotional fuel to keep us headed in the right direction.

Communication With Purpose – Through my years of

helping people on hotlines, I realized God has given me a lot of wisdom and insight on how to help people who are stuck in their problems. Therefore, my communication style is to help them see where they are at in this process, especially the underlying issues, and encourage them and give them guidance on how to live a better life. As a result of me helping others, my life is turned around. Once I determined my Love Language (touch), it helped me understand a lot of the hurts I had in past relationships.

Change My Lifestyle – I had to quit hanging around negative people and purposely seek out like-minded people (Christian and/or entrepreneurial pursuit). With the shutdown from the pandemic it has been harder to be around people. Thus I have diligently sought out leaders on the Internet who can speak encouragement and hope into my life through their online seminars.

Chapter 9

Faith, Hope and Love

> *We activate God's power within us by the words we speak and the actions we take, according to the specific pictures we hold steadfast in our minds, with the ultimate goal of loving God and others.*
> ~Kathy Williamson

What does faith, hope and love have to do with obtaining and maintaining emotional freedom and rebuilding our lives? Everything!

Are we using faith in ourselves to be able to change our lives? Or are we placing our faith in God Who will never fail us? Due to limited space in this book I will discuss a brief overview of how faith, hope and love play an active part in our daily lives.

First, let's look at some descriptions of these three characteristics:

Hope – a positive imagination of God's promises coming into fruition in our lives. If no specific pictures in our imagination, nothing to attach our faith to.

Faith – God has already provided what we need (including healing). But it is in the spiritual realm. Our faith in God is believing that it has already been provided and we speak it forth to bring it into reality. Faith is voice-activated and action-activated. We are not pleading with God to do such-and-such. He has already done it.

Love – our ultimate purpose in life is to love God and others.

Let me paint a picture to help you remember these characteristics. Hopefully everyone knows what a coat rack looks like—a board with coat hooks on it and coats hanging on those hooks. The board is God's love, the hooks are our pictures of hope for specific things, and faith is the coats hanging on the hooks. Without the board, there is nothing to attach the coat hooks to. Without the coat hooks, there is nothing to hang the coats on.

Many people believe if they have enough faith, they can get God to move on their behalf. It's like trying to hang your coat (faith) on the board (God) without any hooks (hope) to keep it there. The Bible says, *Now faith is confidence in what we hope for and assurance about what we do not see* (Hebrews 11:1 NIV). A hook (hope) is a very specific thing. We cannot have generalized faith and expect to get specific results.

Therefore, as we rebuild our lives we need to have specific pictures in our mind of what we want and then we can attach our faith to it and believe (know for certain) that it will come into existence in our physical world. Once we have asked and believed, then we take action while we continually praise God for the provision of it until it becomes a reality in our lives.

When we deal with our emotional overwhelm and desire

to get rid of it, we must have a clear picture of what we want to replace it with. The more we focus on the positive image of our new emotional state, the quicker it comes.

Faith Requires Action

I have discussed a lot in this book about creating new pictures in our minds of what we do want. That is only one part of the equation. We must put actions to our new beliefs. If I am believing God will open doors for employment, then I need to be taking actions to pursue finding that job. I encourage you not to be one of the naysayers who say, "nobody is hiring and I just have to wait until things open up again." You can't afford to allow yourself to stay on the slippery road that leads to doom and destruction.

The Bible indicates that *[Abraham's] faith and his actions were working together, and his faith was made complete by what he did* (James 2:22 NIV, brackets mine). Scriptures show that many times when Jesus was about to heal someone, He asked them to do something physical, such as:

- Then he [Jesus] said to the man, "Stretch out your hand." So he stretched it out and it was completely restored, just as sound as the other (Matthew 12:13 NIV, brackets mine).
- *When he [Jesus] saw them, he said, "Go, show yourselves to the priests." And as they went, they were cleansed* (Luke 7:14 NIV, brackets mine).

There are many more examples. The question for each of us is, what action(s) can we take for each of the things we are believing for? If we are believing for a physical healing, what actions would we be able to do if we were healed? Do those actions now. If we want our underlying emotional blockages removed, what actions would result from them being gone? Do them now. If our emotional overwhelm was gone, what would we be doing? Take action now.

Is God Finicky?

Does God grant some people's requests and ignore others? Does God sometimes heal and most of the time He doesn't? Does God allow (or cause) bad things to happen to us to teach us a lesson? The answer is 'no' to each of these. Let's examine the truth from God's Word.

The Bible states, *If you declare with your mouth, "Jesus is Lord," and believe in your heart that God raised him from the dead, you will be saved. For it is with your heart that you believe and are justified, and it is with your mouth that you profess your faith and are saved* (Romans 10:9-10 NIV). I want to look at the word "saved." The Greek word is *sozo* and it stands for save or saved, made whole, and healed. We believed instantly for our salvation and knew we were saved. However, we weren't taught we also got all these other benefits too.

Therefore a lot of Christians believe they have to convince God to make them whole or to heal them, not realizing that God has already done that. Instead, we need to claim it by faith—speaking forth the truth, followed by appropriate actions, and look for its manifestation in our lives.

A lot of people have been taught that God brings sickness and calamity upon us to teach us a lesson. Earlier in the book I mentioned that several things can bring sickness and calamity into our lives: Satan, decisions by other people, and/or our own decisions. But God does not bring bad things upon us. In John 10:10 it states: *"The thief [Satan] comes only to steal and kill and destroy; I [Jesus] have come that they may have life, and have it to the full"* (NIV, Brackets mine).

Transformation that Sticks

In what areas do you need to change your thoughts and actions to line up with God's truths?

Choose My Destination – Has God called you to something big in your life? This is the destination you need to choose. Then place your total hope and faith in God that it will come into fruition.

Change My Focus – the Bible indicates that what we think about is how we will become. The Word says that as a man thinks, so is he (Proverbs 23:7). If you stay focused on your overwhelm, that is what will continue to show up in your life. When you focus on helping others, your life dramatically changes as a by-product. Proverbs 11:25 (NIV) states: *A generous person will prosper; whoever refreshes others will be refreshed*. This is God's way of changing us.

Control My Emotions – Yes, Tapping (EFT) is a skill that Christians can use too. See the resource in Appendix E for the book *EFT For Christians Advanced: Change Your Feelings, Change Your Life.* Should you desire not to utilize this skill, then believe upon the instructions by Jesus that said, *Do not let your hearts be troubled. You believe in God; believe also in me* (John 14:1 NIV). Jesus would not tell us to not let our hearts be troubled unless we are able to do so

Challenge My Beliefs – Don't take my words as being true. Do your own research of the Scriptures (the Bible) to determine for yourself what is true. The Bible instructs us to do this: *Now the Berean Jews were of more noble character than those in Thessalonica, for they received the message with great eagerness and examined the Scriptures every day to see if what Paul said was true* (Acts 17:11 NIV). Let God's Word guide you to His truth and how it specifically applies to your life.

Clarify Underlying Issues – The bigger picture of what our underlying problems are and where they arise from comes from a passage in Jeremiah:

"Let not the wise boast of their wisdom or the strong boast of their strength or the rich boast of their riches, but let

the one who boasts boast about this: that they have the understanding to know me, that I am the LORD, who exercises kindness, justice and righteousness on earth, for in these I delight," declares the LORD Jeremiah 9:23-24 (NIV).

I am aware that not everyone reading this book professes to be a Christian. Yet I put this particular Scripture here to show a deep underlying issue most people don't recognize.

Communicate With Purpose – A major shift promoted in this book is to reach out to love and help others. This is confirmed by Ephesians 4:29 (NIV): *Do not let any unwholesome talk come out of your mouths, but only what is helpful for building others up according to their needs, that it may benefit those who listen.* Love is the biggest theme throughout the Bible: *let us love one another, for love comes from God. Everyone who loves has been born of God and knows God* (1 John 4:7 NIV). Bring love into every situation and watch God work!

Change My Lifestyle – Faith, hope and love. All three are required to help us walk this path of change. Without them, we get stuck in overwhelm in many areas of our lives, with no hope for permanent change. Remember the coat rack? What are your specific hooks you are believing God will bring into reality? What words to you need to speak, and what actions will show you and others that you believe what you have asked for will come into fruition?

Here is a passage from the Book of Jeremiah that sums up everything pretty good:

This is what the LORD says: "Cursed is the one who trusts in man, who draws strength from mere flesh and whose heart turns away from the LORD. That person will be like a bush in the wastelands; they will not see prosperity when it comes. They will dwell in the parched places of the desert, in a salt land where no one lives.

But blessed is the one who trusts in the LORD, whose confidence is in him. They will be like a tree planted by the water that sends out its roots by the stream. It does not fear when heat comes; its leaves are always green. It has no worries in a year of drought and never fails to bear fruit."

The heart is deceitful above all things and beyond cure. Who can understand it? I the LORD search the heart and examine the mind, to reward each person according to their conduct, according to what their deeds deserve. Jeremiah 17:5-10 (NIV).

Keep this in mind as you learn from the next chapter about how to build a new life.

Chapter 10

How To Build a New Life

> *Now is the time to reset, refocus, rebuild, and raise our sights for living a new, improved life. I CAN—I WILL—WATCH ME!* ~Kathy Williamson

Living in the COVID-19 pandemic has made a lot of us more inward focused, especially due to the personal losses we have encountered. Some people will be able to resume life as usual after the pandemic has ended. Others will not. For many it is a time to reset, refocus, rebuild and raise our sights for living a new, improved life. We have a choice to either stay stuck where we are in our negativity, self-centeredness, *poor me* mentality—or have an attitude that it is possible to change and rise above this reign of fear and uncertainty. Hopefully by now you have regained some hope and confidence for a brighter future, despite the unknown at this time.

Living a Life of Emotional Freedom

Once you choose your new destination, learn new transformational skills, switch your focus to living fully every day, and have developed a new vision for your future—this is your new you. Let's get a little bit more tangible in applying these principles throughout your life. How does everything you have learned in this book translate into real life? We will review this new knowledge in light of the four main pillars of our lives:

- Health
- Wealth
- Love
- Faith

As you go through these four pillars, keep in mind the following typical obstacles that might be standing in your way:

- Limiting beliefs
- Unresolved anger
- Thinking your circumstances are holding you back
- Lack of money
- Lack of resources
- No one to support you
- No written plan
- Undisciplined
- Lack of courage
- You don't know the "how"

Appendix A on Tapping Into Peace has been turned into a free PDF ebook: *Tapping Into Peace and Hope Amid COVID-19: A Better Life Awaits You Today.* That ebook contains excerpts from this book dealing with Tapping on various emotions and issues addressed in this book, including each of the above possible internal obstacles. This PDF ebook was created for you as a quick reference guide. Go to my website to get your free copy: www.EmotionalFreedomFromCOVID19.com.

Health

If you currently have COVID-19 or are a long-hauler struggling with symptoms that won't go away, use Tapping to control your fears and anxieties. In fact, Tapping has also had great success on reducing or eliminating physical symptoms. Remember I am not making any promises for successful elimination of physical symptoms. However, I have used it personally for some physical symptoms and have had some success. And what a relief it is when that symptom disappears quickly!

Since I have not personally had COVID-19, I cannot claim to know the level of fear and anxiety these people may be going through. I have joined a couple of COVID-19 support groups on Facebook and read daily about the struggles from the physical limitations, fears and anxieties, and how the physical symptoms have dramatically affected the quality of their lives. I am also aware that at this time there isn't much out there to help or support the long-haulers. You may wish to join my free Facebook Group https://www.facebook.com/groups/emotionalfreedomfromcovid19/ to receive further teachings from me, as well as encouragement from others, on applying the information in this book and their results.

You may feel the odds are against you. Fear and anxiety have taken over your life. But I am here to encourage you that you *can* beat the odds! Our attitudes determine our ability to move forward to raise ourselves above our circumstances. We cannot let the attitude of defeat develop due to this pandemic and the unknowns about the virus. We must be persistent in our search for better health.

To take control of your health you may need to do your own research on the Internet of what has helped other people recover from or improve the symptoms you struggle with. You must take control of your health and hold strong dialogues with your doctors, discussing the options you found that helped other people with your condition. Remember, even doctors cannot agree on common treatment programs for the virus, and a lot of them are not aware of the symptoms that linger for months. No, it's not *all in your head*!

If your loved one is too sick to stand up for his or her health, then you must be their advocate and do the research and hold the hard discussions with the doctors. This is a new era in medicine that is still being written, and rewriting some of the old processes that no longer work on this type of virus.

We must remain proactive in our efforts to avoid getting the virus. Whatever your beliefs are about wearing face masks and/or putting into place social distancing, the debate is not over and only in hindsight will we recognize what worked and what didn't. For me, I will take whatever measures are necessary to provide a better chance of me not getting the virus. How other people choose to act in preventing their getting the virus is up to them. It is not up to us to force our beliefs upon them. Yes, their actions or inactions may increase the possibility of transmitting the virus, but their decisions are based upon something that is out of our control to change. Let's stay focused on bettering our lives so we can then help others rise to a higher level of living too.

I understand that the steps to prevent getting the virus have turned into a political agenda in the United States. It is not the purpose of this book to look at it from that viewpoint. I want to encourage each person to do what they believe is best for them. However—remember from chapter 5 about challenging our beliefs and be open to the possibility that our beliefs may be false? This is something for all of us to ponder and come to our own decisions, after we have conducted our own valid research in an era of medical confusion about how the virus is transmitted.

Wealth

Financial ruin has struck many people. Once again, the goal of this book is to reduce the emotional overwhelm created by COVID-19, not necessarily resolve the ongoing external circumstances. I am trying to give you some basic structures to think about in your pursuit of life during and after COVID.

Before we can determine options available to increase our financial income, we must get our emotions under control. Without reducing our overwhelm, we will never be in a place to see the possibilities that currently exist.

Being under a very strong financial burden can break the spirit of a person, leading to hopelessness and despair. If that is you, I want to encourage you to pick yourself up, wipe off the mud you collected as you went down the slippery road to nowhere, and raise your head up high. Hope and help are on the way. No person is too far gone that they cannot recover. Will it be easy? No. Will it be worth it? Yes!

In chapter 3, Change My Focus, did you discover and decide what you want to do with your life? Or did you give up, thinking any kind of a bright future is hopeless? Once again, this is a belief that can be changed. Some people will put off pursuing a new life until life's circumstances get better. But we can't wait any longer. It is damaging us to just sit and wait for our conditions to change. It takes action to implement permanent changes. Sometimes massive action!

During times of crisis many new millionaires surface. There is still plenty of money in our society, even though the underlying structure of how it is obtained and distributed has changed. If you explore the history of recessions or societal depressions, you will discover that people had to change their viewpoints about how to obtain money, after having their jobs disappear suddenly. The same can be done in your life. I encourage you to grab pen and paper and identify the intangibles about the job you just lost. What were the things you really enjoyed doing? Can you identify what your unique gifts and talents are that set you apart from others? Now brainstorm about what other types of jobs (still viable in the depressed marketplace) you can utilize those qualities. If you can't determine this, ask someone who knows you to help you come up with some ideas.

It's time to think BIG! Let's get beyond the *survival* mentality.

Love

The good, the bad and the ugly of our relationships have been revealed during this pandemic, whether or not we wanted anyone to see the bad side. We have been faced with our own deficiencies in our abilities to manage well our current relationships and/or develop new ones during this time of isolation and change.

Love is like the mortar that holds bricks together to create a wall or a fence. Without love infused around everything we do, each of the bricks of our life can fall and shatter into a million pieces. COVID has revealed where the mortar is weak in our lives. Some bricks have already broken, others are still repairable. And some spaces require brand new bricks. All encased with a strong bond of love.

Chapter 7 discussed a lot about love, and especially the 5 Love Languages. Understanding these five types of Love Languages and implementing them can dramatically improve your relationships and the love manifested through them.

It's time to look at your life and determine where the love in your relationships got damaged because of the pandemic. Are there people you need to ask them to forgive you for something you did or didn't do? Do you need to forgive others who said or did something that hurt you? If so, the sooner you do these things, the faster the relationships can begin restoration.

It can be very hurtful when relationships fall apart. Some people may escape dealing with their painful emotions by abusing alcohol or drugs. Then they get caught up in a vicious cycle of stopping for a little while, and then relapsing until it becomes an addiction they feel they have no control over. Although I don't have the space here to give a full discourse on how addicts can stop the relapsing, these broken relationships (and/or lack of love) in their lives can be one of many underlying issues (not the alcohol or drugs). Therefore, once these relationships, or the hurt from rejection, etc., are identified and resolved, then the need to escape through one's addiction is gone. And yes, the addiction can be gone forever if they continue to follow the *Roadmaps to Freedom* set forth in this book.

Faith

Our spiritual lives impact every area of our physical lives. We cannot separate our beliefs about God from what's going on in the rest of our lives. Before I discuss how our faith helps us eliminate our emotional overwhelm, there are two areas I need to explain and ask that you then ponder this information.

Who Said God Did It?

When tragedy strikes our lives we sometimes blame God for what's happening. I hear people say, "Why did God allow this to happen to me?" "Why isn't God answering my prayers for healing?" "If God is a good God, then why am I (and so many other people) suffering through this pandemic?"

The first thing to examine is, who said God did this? Our trials and problems come from several sources: the devil, our decisions and actions, and the decisions and actions of others. A lot of people have the misconception that God is in control of everything and, therefore, He is the one allowing this to happen to us. Most of this viewpoint is based upon Scriptures from the Book of Job in the Old Testament where Satan had to ask God permission to inflict Job, because God had a hedge of protection around Job. However, there are many more Scriptures throughout the Bible that show us that man was given free will and God will not override that free will.

Therefore, if a person decides to (accidentally or on purpose) create a new virus, God will not stop him. Should people contract this virus and begin to be around other people, the result is that the virus spreads. Yes, we didn't do anything to willingly catch the virus or be an unknown transmitter of the virus. As indicated earlier, only in hindsight will we know what actions worked to prevent the spread of the virus.

It isn't God sending the virus to punish people or nations. God would love to help you recover from the virus (your physical symptoms), as well as help us recover the losses we encountered in various areas of our lives. Was Satan involved in this? Probably. In John 10:10 it states: *"The thief [Satan] comes only to steal and kill and destroy; I [Jesus] have come that they may have life, and have it to the full"* (NIV, Brackets mine). Were man's decisions involved? Yes. Were our own decisions involved? Possibly. Was God involved? No.

The spiritual world operates by rules and if we do not know those rules, and put them into place then we won't get the results we desire. Space does not permit to give an in-depth discussion of these rules and how to activate your faith to get the results you desire. I recommend the following books (and their accompanying TV teachings) by Bible teacher Andrew Wommack to help you gain a better understanding of God, His love for us, and how God has already provided everything we need to live an abundant life above our circumstances:

- *God Wants You Well – What the Bible Really Says About Walking in Divine Health*
- *You've Already Got It – So Quit Trying To Get It*
- *The Believer's Authority – What You Didn't Learn in*

Church
- *A Better Way to Pray – If Your Prayer Life Is Not Working, Consider Changing Directions*

Andrew Wommack has many more books and teachings available. You can download for free all his TV programs from his Gospel Truth broadcasts going back quite a few years. (www.AWMI.net) It's time for us to become equipped to fight the spiritual battles going on and to rise above our circumstances.

How does our faith help us rebuild our lives? When we have a solid foundation from which to build a new life upon, we have confidence that whatever we put our hands to will succeed. We learn God's promises, the rules of the Kingdom, take daily action to implement what we have learned, and praise God for the results, even before they manifest in our physical world.

Your New Future

Life's challenges never end. What you have learned in this book can be used to get you through future trials in your life. I hope you have gained new knowledge, skills and insights as you went through this book. Now it is up to you to dig deep and determine what needs to be changed in your life, and make the commitment to implement change starting today.

Chapter 11

Daily Rituals For a New You

> *Repetition is the key to permanent change.*
> *~Kathy Williamson*

You just finished reading a new process to help you overcome your emotional overwhelm and build a better life. There is a lot of information to process, but how do we put it into something to remember to do every day? To assist you I have put together some rituals to perform every morning and evening. If you have gone through this book with another person, now is the time to begin to hold each other accountable for implementing these changes. The results will amaze you!

Morning

1. Read my daily affirmations (new beliefs to reduce emotions / to instill hope for my future) while Tapping.
2. Anybody I didn't forgive yesterday? Forgive them now.
3. Review and visualize myself doing my main goal today that will propel me into fulfilling my vision.
4. Visualize myself accomplishing my vision. What are

my feelings, emotions? Whose lives did I impact? Review your Vision Board.
5. What kind of involvement can I intentionally have today with my family/friends?
6. How can I intentionally show love and encouragement to others today? What specific actions or words will I use?
7. Review my planner for the activities scheduled for today.

Evening

1. Review how well I handled my emotions today. How could I handle some of them differently in the future? What were the thoughts behind the emotions? What different thoughts can I use in the future to avoid becoming negative?
2. Is there anybody I need to forgive for what was said or done to me today? Forgive them now.
3. Do I need to reach out to ask for forgiveness from someone I might have hurt today? If so, when will I do that (specific date/time)?
4. Did I accomplish my one main goal today? If not, what thoughts or excuses kept me from doing it?
5. What thoughts or inactions do I need to do Tapping on? Do it now.
6. What am I grateful for in my life in general and from today's activities?
7. What is one main goal (personal or business) for tomorrow that will make me be excited when I wake up? Visualize myself doing the actions to carry it out.

I encourage you to share your results in my private Facebook Group "Emotional Freedom From COVID-19." This group is a place to share your struggles and successes in implementing change, ask questions, and receive encouragement from like-minded people, as well as myself.

Chapter 12

Words of Encouragement

I CAN — I WILL — WATCH ME!

To get through uncharted waters during our time in this pandemic requires courage, perseverance, and a "can do" attitude. These times will test our faith, uncover where our weak points are in the foundations of our lives, and we will either thrive or get sucked into a struggle so deep we won't know what to do.

Hopefully your attitude has improved after reading this book, answering the many questions, and taking a deep inventory of what you want in life. I have been praying for you that you soak in this new knowledge and integrate it into your daily life.

Nobody is beyond hope nor are circumstances too bad that they can't be changed. However, we cannot forget our history and must keep those lessons in front of us. Everything has a limited course to run. The pandemic will not last forever. Societies will reopen and businesses will begin their pursuit to grow and thrive. Families will reconnect and relationships flourish once again.

Grief and sorrows will run their course and the sun will shine again in our lives on a daily basis. We will be stronger and more resilient because of surviving this pandemic. But it won't happen automatically.

A better life never happens without our being intentional to pursue it.

This pandemic has forced us to isolate, but let's not get too comfortable being alone. Man was created for interaction with others, which creates the spice in life. As we begin to rebuild our lives, let's not be so self-centered that we forget to reach out to love and help others. That will be the key to giving us the motional fuel to continue along the right path for us.

I encourage you to join me on our private Facebook group where you can receive further teachings from me, as well as encouragement from others, on applying the information in this book and their results.

https://www.facebook.com/groups/emotionalfreedomfromcovid19/

If you need a quick video overview of the contents of this book, go to

www.EmotionalFreedomFromCOVID19.com/overview.

With God all things are possible! (Matthew 19:26 NIV)

Appendix A

Tapping Into Peace

PREFACE

Disclaimer

Please read the following Disclaimer pertaining to the skill of Tapping before proceeding further.

The information presented in this book, including ideas, suggestions, exercises, techniques, and other materials, is educational in nature and is provided only as general information and is not medical or psychological advice. This book is solely intended for the reader's own self-improvement and is not meant to be a substitute for medical or psychological treatment and does not replace the services of licensed health care professionals.

This book contains information regarding an innovative healing method called Tapping (also known as Emotional Freedom Technique or EFT), which is considered part of the field of complementary and alternative medicine. Tapping seeks to address stressors and imbalances within a person's energy system, as well as the energetic influence of thoughts, beliefs, and emotions on the body. Tapping is intended to balance an individual's energy with a gentle tapping procedure. The prevailing premise of Tapping is that the flow and balance of the body's electromagnetic and more subtle energies are important for physical, spiritual, and emotional health, and for fostering well-being.

Although Tapping appears to have promising emotional, spiritual, and physical health benefits, Tapping has yet to be fully researched by the Western academic, medical, and psychological communities. Therefore, Tapping may be considered experimental. The reader agrees to assume and accept full responsibility for any and all risks associated with reading this book and using Tapping. If the reader has any concerns or questions about whether or not to use Tapping, the reader should consult with his or her licensed health care professional. If the reader inadvertently experiences any emotional distress or physical discomfort in using Tapping, the reader is advised to stop and seek professional care if appropriate.

Publishing of the information contained in this book is not intended to create a client-practitioner or any other type of professional relationship between the reader and the author. The author does not make any guarantee that the reader will receive or experience the same results described in this book. Further, the author does not make any guarantee, warranty, or prediction regarding the outcome of an individual using Tapping as described herein for any particular purpose or issue. While references and links to other resources are provided in good faith, the accuracy, validity, effectiveness, completeness, or usefulness of any information herein, as with any publication, cannot be guaranteed.

By continuing to read this book, the reader agrees to forever fully release, indemnify, and hold harmless, the author, and others associated with the publication of this book from any claim or liability and for any damage or injury of whatsoever kind or nature that the reader may incur, arising at any time, out of or in relation to the reader's use of the information presented in this book. If any court of law rules that any part of this Disclaimer is invalid, the Disclaimer stands as if those parts are struck out.

BY CONTINUING TO READ THIS BOOK YOU AGREE TO ALL OF THE ABOVE.

* * * * * * *

Tapping is a simple five-minute technique for removing unwanted emotions. Tapping has helped many people who have been stuck for years in painful memories, fears, anxieties, insecurities, and even physical pain. Many studies have proven that it effectively reduces emotional states. This modality has been approved by the Veterans Administration as part of their program to assist Vets dealing with PTSD and other mental issues. For further information on the research and the proven benefits of Tapping, check out www.TheTappingSolution.com. Nick Ortner, New York Times Best-Selling Author, also provides an app you can download for free (www.TheTappingSolutionApp.com).

Tapping (EFT) can be classified as energy psychology. This classification deters many Christians from being open to use it, thinking it is New Age theology. My belief is this is a tool which has no spiritual bias towards evil and, therefore, it can be used to enhance our spiritual growth in our relationship with God. I am a Christian and as I do my tapping, I add phrases from the Bible that relate to the issue I am tapping on. If you are a Christian I encourage you to integrate Scriptures with Tapping for the best and quickest way to leaning into God's peace and joy. See Appendix E for the resource book *EFT For Christians Advanced*.

Quickest Way to Positive, Lasting Change

It's hard to make positive changes in your lifestyle when you've got anxieties and out-of-control emotions running your life. Perhaps you know what you need to do to change, but you can't make the transition because all your unresolved internal triggers show up to stop you. If you don't know how to eliminate them, you stay stuck.

Imagine what your life would look like if you had a skill to help you deal with those anxieties and emotions the moment they came up. You could take back control of your life. You no longer need to allow your negative emotions to overwhelm you. You can then take massive action steps with confidence. Your dreams are no longer out of reach!

This one tool can help you:

- Handle the anxieties that creep into your life.
- Control your emotions.
- Identify and change your negative thoughts.
- Improve your confidence.
- Overcome your hurts from your past.
- Replace your negative self-talk with positive thoughts.
- Stretch out of your comfort zone to take new actions to change.
- Pursue your vision for your life with gusto!

I suggest you write down the issues, behaviors, or thoughts that you see need changed in your life immediately. Now prioritize them according to which one should be dealt with first because it will have the most impact upon your daily life.

The Tapping Process

Choose one emotion or problem you want to Tap on. Sometimes you just have the emotion and don't know what is causing it. Before you start, identify the intensity of your emotional issue on a scale of 1 to 10, with 1 being the lowest intensity and 10 is the highest intensity. You will check this level again after you have done several rounds of Tapping.

Below is a diagram that shows the tapping points on the body. You will use your fingertips to gently tap on each of these points 6-7 times before proceeding to the next point. Use your index finger and your middle finger to do the Tapping. When you do the Setup Phrase below, use these fingers to tap on the Karate Chop point on your opposite hand.

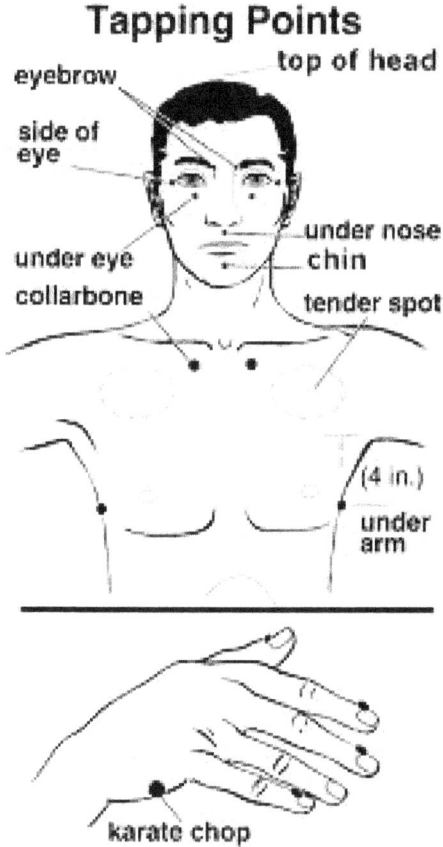

The Setup Phrase

The purpose of the Setup Phrase is to identify the problem or label the emotion, and to also accept yourself even though you have this problem. While continuously tapping the Karate Chop point on the side of the hand (see the diagram above), speak out loud the following statement three times:

Even though I'm upset about _____ (name the problem),[or, I'm feeling anxious about],

I deeply and completely accept myself and love myself.

The Tapping Sequence

Tap about 6-7 times (estimate) on each of the energy points on the above diagrams, while repeating a brief phrase that reminds you of the problem. I'll give you a quick example and then examples that apply to the seven emotional states listed in chapter 2.

Here's the Sequence:

- Eyebrow (inner part of your eyebrow where it starts in the center of your head)
- Side of the eye
- Under your eye
- Under your nose
- Your chin (the indentation part of your chin)
- Your collarbone
- Under your arm
- Top of the head in the center

Here's a quick example:

Karate Chop: *Even though I'm very anxious right now, I deeply and completely love myself and accept myself.* Repeat this two more times before moving on to tapping on the other meridian points.

As you go through the tapping cycle, just continue to repeat the shorter phrases and/or related phrases. You don't have to say the same phrase for each tapping point. You can change the wording as you feel fit. When you see the ellipses ... move to the next tapping point.

Even though I'm anxious, I accept myself ... I'm very anxious but don't know why ... It's okay for this anxiety to go away ... I don't need this anxiety any longer ... Whatever I am anxious about is not real ... This anxiety has to go ... I can handle my life without this anxiety ... I can handle whatever situation is before me without getting anxious.

After you have done this tapping round twice, evaluate on a scale of 0-10 your emotional state. If it has not decreased to a 3 or lower, continue doing more rounds.

Tail Enders

When you tap, you may have objections come up in your thoughts. In fact, these may be your main problem. The objections can start out with "yes, but ...," "that won't work in my life because ...," "I tried to do this, but I failed ...," "these negative statements are true and I can't change them ...." It's very important that you acknowledge these tail enders and use Tapping to resolve them. If they are not resolved, they may hinder the effectiveness of your Tapping to lower your emotional state.

Repeat as Needed

After you have gone through the tapping sequence two or three times, stop and reassess where you are. Before you started you assessed where your emotional intensity was on a scale of 0-10. Now where are you at? If you still have some negative emotions, then repeat as follows:

Setup Phrase: *Even though I still have some remaining negative feelings about _____ (the problem), I deeply and completely love and accept myself.*

Tapping Points: *Even though I still have some negative emotions about _____, I accept myself.* And keep repeating some of the statements you used in your previous sequence or add new ones as you go through this tapping sequence.

Sometimes when you tap on one of these physical points, you may feel an instant relief from your emotions. If so, you might want to continue tapping on that specific physical point as you finish your sequence of statements.

Let's Reduce Your Emotional State Now

Frontliners:

If you are a frontliner, here are special Tapping sequences for you to use.

Your 10-minute break

Set-up Phrase: *Even though I am physically and emotionally exhausted, I completely love myself and accept myself* (repeat two more times).

I release my physical exhaustion ... I relax and allow more energy to fill me up ... I will continue to work at my best for the rest of my shift ... I release my exhaustion ... I relax my muscles ... I'm taking a few deep breaths to renew myself ... I receive this new physical energy ... I can do this.

I release my emotional overwhelm ... the facts are what they are ... yes I may have seen a lot of sad things ... even death ... and I release my emotional overwhelm over these facts ... I choose to continue to believe I am making a difference in these people's lives ... even if they are unable to verbally tell me ... I know my heart is in the right place.

Even though I deal with this physical and emotional exhaustion every day ... I know my presence and my skills are impacting these people's lives ... I choose to believe that my life is impacting others ... I know my heart loves these people ... and I just want the best for each person ... I choose to be the hope for the person who has lost hope ... I choose to convey love to each person and his or her family ... I choose to be a beacon of hope and light in this dark pandemic.

Physical Exhaustion

Set-up Phrase: *Even though I am physically exhausted, I completely love myself and accept myself (repeat two more times).*

I am physically exhausted ... I don't know how much longer I can work today ... I need relief ... I release my anxiety over this exhaustion ... I release my fears of making mistakes because I'm physically exhausted ... I release my fears of making mistakes ... I release my exhaustion ... I receive new energy to continue working.

Even though I am physically exhausted ... these few moments by myself will bring relief ... I turn my focus away from my exhaustion ... and I receive an influx of physical energy ... so I can continue my work today ... and provide my best to help these patients ... I release my exhaustion ... I receive new energy to continue working.

Emotional Overwhelm

Set-up Phrase: *Even though I am emotionally overwhelmed, I completely love myself and accept myself (repeat two more times).*

I am so emotional ... watching these people suffer ... and I can't fix them ... it is just so hard ... to see so many people suffer ... and I know some of them won't make it ... even though I try my hardest ... it's just not enough.

I release my emotional overwhelm ... I release my anxieties ... there are so many people to help ... and too few of us to do an adequate job ... I release my emotions of panic ... feeling inadequate at times ... at times wondering whether all my efforts make any difference ... I release my emotional overwhelm.

I am astonished at the viewpoints of some patients ... seeing them flat-out deny what they are going through ... it makes me angry ... and sad ... that they won't acknowledge the truth about this virus ... I release my anger ... I release my sadness ... I can't change their attitudes.

I feel isolated in my emotional overwhelm ... anybody outside my profession doesn't know what I'm going through ... I feel so alone in this battle ... my family doesn't totally understand the stress I am under ... I release my feelings of isolation ... I release my need for others to fully understand what I'm going through ... I accept my calling to do this work ... I release my pent-up emotions.

No End in Sight

Set-up Phrase: Even though I am exhausted and I don't know when this virus will settle down or go away, I completely love myself and accept myself (repeat two more times).

Even though I work my butt off every day under high stress ... and I don't know how much longer I need to work under these conditions ... I choose to take it one day at a time ... I release my anxieties over getting burnout ... I release my anxieties over getting the virus ... I choose to believe ... I have the physical and mental abilities to work under this stress ... and my immune system will stay in great shape to keep me safe.

In chapter 2 we discussed various emotional states you could be in currently. Here are examples of Tapping sequences to use for each.

1. Emotionally—Grief

Set-up Phrase: Even though I am grieving over _____ (describe), I completely love myself and accept myself.

This grieving is so overwhelming ... I'm not sure how to get through the day ... My emotions are so out of whack ... It's okay for me to grieve ... I won't be forgetting why I'm grieving ... I just need to reduce the level of intensity of my emotions right now ... It's okay ... I'm okay.

It's okay to grieve over (describe – death of a loved one) ... I don't want to forget what happened ... But I want my emotions to reduce right now ... I know that person would want me to move on with my life ... It's okay for me to treasure his/her life and move on ... (person's name) will remain in my memory ... Even though the level of the intensity of grief goes down ... Thank you (person's name) for being part of my life and I will see you again some day.

2. Emotionally—Anger/Fears Over

Set-up Phrase: Even though I am angry over _____ (describe), I completely love myself and accept myself. [Example is anger over loss of connection with relatives and society.]

Even though I am forced to physically isolate ... I release my anger for this situation ... I know it is only temporary ... Even if I don't know for how long ... but I will maintain my social distancing to avoid getting the virus or passing along the virus ... Even though I am angry that I no longer have complete control over my schedule ... I choose to release that anger ... I choose to live in peace.

I am fearful of more limitations being placed on my freedom ... I release that fear ... I can handle whatever is going on in my life ... I do have personal freedoms that I will stand up for ... and I let go of my fear that these limitations will become permanent ... It's okay to stand up for my constitutional rights ... but I will also be proactive to not spread the virus ... I release my fears.

3. Physically—Loss of

Set-up Phrase: Even though I am physically limited and cannot do _____ (describe), I completely love myself and accept myself.

Although I am cooped up in my house ... I completely love myself and accept myself ... I choose to not focus on the negative of this situation ... but to find positive things I can do during this isolation ... Every day I choose to have a positive outlook on life ... I choose to work on building an awesome future ... if I can find a way to reach people online, show me ... I will adapt to this new living situation.

[For mothers with children] Even though my kids are driving me crazy ... I completely love myself and accept myself ... I choose to let go of my desire to keep everything perfect and in order ... and realize the children are under this extra stress too ... I hereby release my stress ... I release my need to control ... I accept my situation ... because I know it is only temporary.

4. Health (COVID Sufferers – Current and Long-Haulers)

Set-up Phrase: Even though I am terrified because I have this virus, I completely accept myself and love myself.

My anxiety is so high ... I'm ready to let it go ... But I have all these fears ... Fear of not knowing how bad it will get for me ... Fear I might die ... Fear of being away from my loved ones during this time due to enforced quarantine ... Fear of having long-term symptoms ... Fear of not knowing what to expect.

I have pre-existing medical conditions and I am afraid ... I hear about so many people in my condition dying ... and I am afraid ... I'm ready to let go of my fear ... I know it only aggravates my condition ... I'm ready to live and not die ... I'm ready to dream for a brighter future ... I will survive!

[Long-Haulers] My doctor didn't tell me these symptoms would last so long ... I'm upset that I'm still sick ... I'm afraid because I don't know when my symptoms will go away, if ever ... Nobody understands me ... My doctors tell me 'it's all

in my head' ... It's not all in my head! ... I release my anxiety ... I choose to remain calm.

There is so much fighting going on between doctors and politicians ... and they still don't have a cure for what we're going through ... it makes me angry that very few people in the media are talking about us long-haulers ... I feel forgotten and tossed aside ... I choose to release my anger right now ... I choose to believe my symptoms are clearing up right now ... I'm grateful for the support I receive from other long-haulers ... I choose to focus on my vision for my future rather than get stuck in this emotional overwhelm.

Long-haulers: I suggest you find support groups for COVID on Facebook to receive further emotional support from others in your situation.

I suggest you do Tapping on each of your physical symptom, addressing your fear about it, commanding it to be healed, and believe it will happen.

5. Financial – Loss of

Set-up Phrase: Even though I have anxiety over _____ (describe), I completely love myself and accept myself. [Example is for person's inability to provide for their loved ones.]

I am so angry right now, I don't know what to do ... I've tried everything I can think of to get more money ... It's just not there ... I'm so angry and overwhelmed, I don't know what to do ... I feel like a failure ... I am a failure ... I've let my family down ... I don't see any way out.

Even though I can't see a way out ... I know this pandemic will pass ... I believe something will open up for me soon ... I will humble myself and utilize the resources available for food and shelter ... I will let go of my pride and ask for help from others ... Please show me and guide me to what I need ... I release my anger and fears ... I know for certain things will turn around soon.

6. Relationships—Loss of

Set-up phrase: Even though I have lost my peace in my relationships, I completely love myself and accept myself.

This isolation has made me very irritable ... I have lost my peace in my relationships ... I choose to release my anger and anxieties and fears ... I choose to live in peace ... Which may mean having to learn a different way to relate to my loved ones ... I release my being in a bad mood ... and choose to have a brighter outlook on life ... I choose to love others first.

I lost my peace because I'm more focused on myself than others ... I choose to forgive myself for this ... I release my anxieties and fears ... I choose to listen to my loved ones and friends better ... I choose to live in peace ... Even though society is changing ... I know I can adapt and live a happy and prosperous life ... I choose love over fear.

7. Spiritually—Potential Losses

Set-up Phrase: Even though I've lost the physical connection of going to church and being around other Christians, I completely love myself and accept myself.

Even though I've lost the peace and calmness I got from attending church ... I completely love myself ... I am angry that my rights to attend church are being hindered by the government (in U.S.) ... I know there is a pandemic ... and my desire to worship in church is being dampened ... I choose to remain in peace ... I choose to turn toward God ... to receive His peace and joy.

Although the structure for my spiritual growth is temporarily gone ... I choose to find new ways to study God's Word ... and draw close to God ... I release my anger over this situation ... I choose to take full responsibility for my spiritual growth ... I choose to draw even closer to God ... I will not let Satan defeat me just because I cannot attend church ... I am a warrior in Christ!

Hope For Building a New Life

Chapter 10 discussed how a person can build a new life during and after this pandemic. While Tapping is used mainly to reduce emotions, it can also be used to instill hope for a better future. If we didn't have any internal triggers, issues or blockages, we would all be living the life of our dreams. Because our beliefs, thoughts and the things we visualize eventually become our reality, we must deal with eliminating the internal processes that stop us from believing and moving forward to fulfill our dreams.

The four pillars of our lives were discussed: Health, Wealth, Love, and Faith. The following are typical internal obstacles that might be standing in our way:

- Limiting beliefs
- Unresolved anger
- Thinking our circumstances are holding us back
- Lack of money
- Lack of resources
- No one to support us
- No written plan
- Undisciplined
- Lack of courage
- We don't know the "how"

In order to build a new life, we must instill new beliefs that support us. It is only when we begin walking a new path do our objections show up. We can dream and visualize all we want, but it is in taking action that we build up our new confidence and hope.

When you developed a new plan for your life in each of the above four pillars, did you write down the action steps to get you there? A key point to remember is that success comes from following and implementing a series of steps that others have proven work. It is not our worthiness, or lack thereof, that determines our success. Yes, we may need to learn new knowledge, skills and character traits to implement, but anything is possible. Yes—even for you!

To beat the odds and come away from this pandemic a thriver, we must take the right actions daily. We must believe that we already have inside us whatever it takes to motivate us and push us forward into a new, awesome life! Let's take a few minutes to go over some Tapping sequences for each of the above possible internal obstacles. The problem with our obstacles being internal is we may not know which ones are the driving force that stop us from moving forward. You might want to go through each tapping sequence, even if you are not sure that it applies to you.

Limiting Beliefs

When you feel an internal hesitancy to start something new, or fear that it won't work out like you want it to, then tap on that situation. It could be regarding your ability to do a particular task, your lack of worthiness to succeed, the pictures of failing at this task in the past holding you back, feeling insecure at trying something new, etc.

Set-up Phrase: *Even though I'm not sure of what my limiting beliefs are regarding _____ , I completely love myself and accept myself.* (Repeat two more times.) [Example is to reach out to strangers to develop new relationships.]

Even though I am hesitant to talk to strangers ... it's okay if I do ... Even if they reject me ... it's okay ... I won't die from embarrassment ... There are plenty of people who will like me ... I am not a bad person ... In fact, I have something special to offer in relationships.

Any memories from embarrassing moments from my past

... I hereby release ... That was a different time and place ... It's okay to release my emotions tied to that event ... Today I have my prepared questions ready to start a conversation ... If I keep the focus on them ... then I won't be afraid ... I will listen and allow them to talk and talk ... and I will feel so relaxed from the beginning.

Unresolved Anger

Sometimes we are angry and have no idea why. We can be angry at life in general or over circumstances or people who have hurt us. We can even be angry at ourselves for numerous reasons. In today's pandemic there are plenty of things to be angry about: being forced into isolation, having our freedom to roam about restricted, loss of finances, loss of our health, etc. If we were an angry person before the pandemic began, it may have heightened our anger or we could have tried to suppress it, only to have it pop up at unexpected times. It is difficult to build a new life with unresolved anger percolating inside us.

Set-up Phrase: *Even though I'm angry over _____ , I completely love myself and accept myself.* (Repeat two more times.) [Example is over so many changes made in short period of time, without knowing when things will get back to normal.]

Even though I've lost my peace ... it's okay ... I choose to restore peace in my life ... I let go of everything that is causing me to be angry ... I let go of my desire to control everything in my life ... I let go of my high expectations of myself and everyone else ... I release my anger over people ... I release my anger over circumstances I can't control.

Even though I have a lot of anger inside me ... I choose to forgive people and circumstances that are affecting me ... I choose to live in peace ... I release any anger against myself ... I forgive myself ... and choose to live a better life ... I choose to love and help others around me ... I choose peace.

My Circumstances Are Holding Me Back

Blaming our circumstances for why we are where we are is the easiest escape route from personal responsibility. We've all heard stories where two people, faced with the exact set of negative circumstances, responded completely opposite. One survived. One didn't. Why? It is our choice on how to interpret and respond to life around us. It is true that because of the pandemic our choices in many areas of our lives are limited, but let's think outside the box in all areas where we feel restricted.

Set-up Phrase: *Even though I blame my circumstances for _____, I completely love myself and accept myself.* (Repeat two more times.) [Example is a mother who had to quit her job to homeschool her children.]

Even though I have had to quit my job to homeschool my children ... I accept this new role ... I set aside my anger at having to quit a job I liked ... a job that had great potential ... a job we needed to financially make ends meet ... and I embrace this new season in my life ... yes, it is just a new season ... not the end of my career.

Even though I was forced into this new season ... I release my feelings of anger ... I release my frustration over my kid's behavior... I release my anger at myself for not doing very well in this new role I never planned for ... I accept my new set of circumstances ... I embrace the new opportunities to love my child ... I will learn new skills to help my child and I to draw closer in our relationship ... I will not blame my circumstances ... but see them as new, exciting opportunities.

Lack of Money

This internal blockage is prolific. Sometimes we are not aware of the false underlying belief that sets us up for failure around obtaining and keeping money. The good thing about

Tapping is we don't always need to know the exact issue in order for Tapping to be effective. Our ability to think outside the box plays a big role in building a new life. If you lost your job during the pandemic, is there some aspect of what you did (or maybe something entirely new) that you can turn into a business online? Find someone to brainstorm with about possible avenues of new income. In the meantime, tap to clear any underlying issues you may have.

Set-up Phrase: *Even though I lack money to _____ , I completely love myself and accept myself.* (Repeat two more times.) [Example is lack of money due to loss of job, and lack of ideas on how to obtain it.]

Even though I lack money ... I release the stress around this ... I let go of my panic from not having enough money ... I release any underlying issue that is stopping me from seeing the opportunities around me ... I open my eyes to see possibilities to make money now ... I release my anxiety over my lack of money ... I choose to live in peace knowing that things will work out ... I release my stress.

Even though I don't know how to make more money ... I choose to believe there is something I can do to make money ... I release any limitations I have on my ability to make money now ... I choose to take responsibility for my life ... rather than allow my circumstances to dictate what I can or cannot do ... I choose to rise higher than my current situation ... and become the type of person I need to be ... to provide for myself and my family.

Lack of Resources

If all we focus on is the empty glass, we will be blind to see the resources available to us. In this time of living in a pandemic, and due to possible lower income levels, our ability to provide for our basic needs may be hindered. I remember the first time I had to go get a food box from the local outlet and how I felt embarrassed, ashamed and mad at myself because I couldn't buy my own food. But I also wanted to eat. I had to let go of my pride.

However, as we look at lack of resources as it pertains to building a new life, it can cover a variety of things. Not only could food be lacking, but also the knowledge, skills, and guidance to help us lay a new path to walk in life. What do you think are the resources you lack? Utilize Tapping to ease your anxiety over that lack and to open your eyes to locate the resources you need to carry out the new vision for your life.

Set-up Phrase: *Even though I lack resources to _____ , I completely love myself and accept myself.* (Repeat two more times.) [Example is lack of resources to help me identify how to start a business online.]

Even though I don't know how to start to build an online business ... I recognize my limited thinking ... but I am willing to expand to consider many ideas ... because I know there is a way for me to move forward in life ... I will not let my lack of resources stop me from moving forward ... I will not let my limited thinking stop me from exploring new ideas ... I am willing to look at new options in life ... I am willing to take risks on something new.

Even though I have a new vision for my life ... I don't believe I have the resources to move forward ... but I am open to finding those resources ... or alternative paths that will work ... so I can move forward starting today ... I will no longer ... sit around doing nothing ... because I think I don't have what it takes to move forward.

No One to Support Me

When we get a new vision for our life, we think everyone will be excited to hear about it and they will support us. Not true! Especially family members and close friends. Then we get disappointed because they want to dampen our dreams, or just don't care. Where do we turn to get that support? Many give up at that point and never try. They take their dreams to the grave and never really live. I don't want that to happen to you. There are ways to get support for our dreams. Especially now that so much business has gone online. Through the Internet we can find people, groups and businesses who will dream with us and support us as we build our dream life. Caution: be aware that some people are just out for your money, so be sure you have a written plan on where you want to go and the skills and knowledge you need to get there. Many free groups exist on Social Media around your topic of interest. There is never a reason to give up for lack of support!

Set-up Phrase: *Even though I don't have anyone to support me around _____, I completely love myself and accept myself.* (Repeat two more times.) [Example is lack of support to start an online business.]

Even though I feel lost on how to start an online business ... I completely love myself and accept myself ... The hurt I felt from lack of encouragement from family and friends ... I release that hurt ... I refuse to let their negative words or lack of encouragement pull me down ... I know I can open a business online ... and I am able to find people to encourage me along this new path ... Yes, I can do this!

Even though I have a big dream ... I lack the day-to-day encouragement to keep me going strong ... But I will find the people who will inspire me ... People who can show me that I can reach my goals ... That success is based upon repeatable skills and practices ... and not on my personal character ... or how I may feel unworthy of accomplishing such a big vision for my life ... Because since others have done what I want to do, so can I!

No Written Plan

When we hear someone talk about writing down a plan, we might think it applies only to a business plan. But what about a plan that covers all four pillars in our lives: Health, Wealth, Love, and Faith? Most of us just 'wing it' in those areas. Yet there are many ways we can write out plans on how to accomplish our goals in each area. Health—plans to eat better and exercise so many days a week. Wealth—plans for a certain level of income, ways to save money on your budget, and start a savings account. Love—ways to determine your spouse's Love Language (see chapter 7 of my book) and plan ways to show them love. Faith—plans to study the Bible, schedule prayer time for yourself and with others, schedule times to call friends and encourage them. Is it time to write your plan for each of the four pillars?

Set-up Phrase: *Even though I don't have a written plan for _____ , I completely love myself and accept myself.* (Repeat two more times.) [Example is for no plan on how to reach out to love and help others during this time of isolation and social restrictions.]

Even though I have been so focused on 'me, myself and I' ... I choose to create a plan on how to reach out to love and help others ... I release my focus only on myself ... I release my anxiety over my own isolation ... I choose to spend 'x' amount of time reaching out to others ... to show them love and to encourage them ... I will reach out to [names] at least ['x' times a week] to encourage them ... If they have prayer requests ... I will write them down to pray over them.

Even though I am busy trying to handle things in my life ... I choose to take time to reach out to love and help others ... I choose to follow my written plan for this ... Because I know that it will benefit me more than it benefits them ... and that what I do for others ... will also be done for me ... I will also receive love and encouragement ... as a by-product of helping others.

Undisciplined

When we try to do something new it takes time to develop new habits that will take us where we want to go in life. If we were undisciplined before this pandemic hit, it makes it even harder to get the momentum going to pull us into a brighter future. However, discipline is a habit that can be learned. We need to decide what we need to be disciplined about. Living in isolation and social distancing has shown us where our weaknesses are and possibly increased our frustrations in that area. Not only do we need to create new habits of discipline, but also stop the negative habits that hold us back. Make a list of new habits you need, and the old habits you wish to eliminate. Choose the one that will have the most impact on your life and do Tapping on that one first.

Set-up Phrase: *Even though I am undisciplined in _____ , I completely love myself and accept myself.* (Repeat two more times.) [Example is for lack of discipline in limiting my time on the Internet and/or my cell phone.]

Even though I spend too much time on the Internet ... I choose to implement a new habit ... A habit of limiting myself to one-half hour on my phone or computer Internet 'x' times a day ... I choose to replace this time by doing _____ [look at your written plan(s) you created previously] ... And if I get stuck starting that project ... I will do Tapping to overcome that fear or hesitancy ... I choose to take the path to a better future ... even in times of massive changes in society.

Even though I enjoy playing games on my phone ... playing games is not helping me move forward in life ... I choose to take action toward my goals ... and be disciplined to take action daily ... The good feelings I get from taking massive actions ... will keep me motivated to continue along that path ... to be disciplined ... even if I have never been disciplined in this area before.

Lack of Courage

Courage is the ability to do something that frightens you. This issue of lack of courage can arise from having any of the above internal obstacles we just discussed. One of the issues not discussed yet is the fear of failure, which also results in a lack of courage. Low self-esteem plays a big part too. When we think, *what will others think about me if I do this*, or *I don't know if this will work for me*, we are focusing only on 'me, myself and I.' But when we switch our focus to *I will do this because I know it will help so many other people*, it removes our hesitancy and builds up our courage. We can also gain courage by reading about other people who did what we want to do and were quite successful at it. Pretty soon we build up ourselves to believe, *if they did it, so can I*. Courage can also be relieved by gaining new knowledge around what we are fearful to do. Knowledge on how to do it correctly so we don't fail. Knowledge to know what positive outcome is on the other side of the action we fear to take. And knowledge that it will work, no matter who tries it. What do you need courage for today?

Set-up Phrase: *Even though I lack courage to _____ , I completely love myself and accept myself.* (Repeat two more times.) [Example is for lack of courage to live my dream life.]

Even though I lack courage to pursue my dream life ... I completely love and accept myself ... I release my fears of what others might think about my dreams ... I release my anxiety over needing others to approve of my dreams ... I release my own doubts about being able to make my dreams come true ... I will pursue the knowledge and skills I need to make my dreams a reality ... I will find the right people to encourage me to fulfill my dreams ... I will live my dreams!

Even though others may laugh at my dreams ... I accept

my bold dreams . . . I accept responsibility for making them come true ... I do have the courage to push through whatever fears show up during this pursuit ... My dreams are worth fighting for ... To have the courage to make them happen ... To set aside my insecurities ... and to take massive action every day toward my dreams!

You Don't Know the "How"

A lot of things in our lives got turned upside down during this pandemic. To build a new life requires that we know "how" to do that. But what if we don't know the "how?" Hopefully after reading my book you have come up with a detailed plan on what your vision is for all four pillars of your life. But there are so many nuances along this new route to successfully reach your awesome destiny. As you run into the unknowns along the path, Tapping will help relieve the anxieties and open your eyes to new possibilities.

Set-up Phrase: *Even though I don't know all the steps to successfully _____ , I completely love myself and accept myself.* (Repeat two more times.) [Example is for releasing any objections to starting to build a new life.]

Even though I don't see how I can get started on doing anything new in my life ... I completely love myself and accept myself ... I release any hesitancies I have to try something new ... I release any fears I have to go after my dreams for my life ... I release all my questions of "how?" for each new thing ... I will get started today ... Even though I don't know the total process ... I will allow myself to flow with what happens as I step out in faith.

Even though I think I know what direction to take ... I give up my control over the process ... And I will allow new possibilities to come my way ... I release my fears that this new adventure won't work out ... I open myself to learn new skills ... I release any negative attitude I might have toward trying something new ... I will pursue this new course until success breaks through ... I will beat the odds and be the awesome person I was created to be!

* * * * * * *

The above are examples to get you started in relieving your emotional overwhelm. I will share more examples through my website www.EmotionalFreedomFromCOVID19.com. Continue to check the website for new updates.

Appendix B

Forgiveness Brings Freedom

Forgiveness sometimes can be an hourly or a daily process. Most people are not taught that once you forgive, you need to commit to never bring up that episode again—either verbally or in your thoughts. Without this step, you end up rehashing how you were hurt in your past (even if it was this morning) and how you were done wrong (the victim mentality).

Are you holding on to anger and hurt from how COVID-19 has impacted your life? You may *feel* that you're not ready to forgive the people who made the decisions that have dramatically changed your life. However, you can't let your feelings make decisions for you. This act of forgiveness isn't for the benefit of those who hurt you, it's for you. If you wait until your feelings tell you it's time to forgive him or her, you will be waiting a long time, as well as wasting a lot of your life that could be lived from a better place of peace and purpose.

Forgiveness Brings Freedom

To turn our focus from the past, or from today's problems, to the future requires us to let go of some of the ugly stuff we've been hanging on to for many years, or even just the last few months. Without forgiveness, we will always have a string tied to our past, holding us back from reaching the fulfilled, purpose-filled life.

"I will never forgive him until he pays for what he did to me!" These words spew out of our mouths and turn our stomachs into knots. We carry a grudge (known as bitterness), sometimes for years, and wonder why we can't enjoy life. Our tendency is to rehash the wrong that was done to us, not for the purpose of designing retaliation, but because it feels good to do so. While the person who hurt us carries on with his or her life unaware of our grudge, we let our bitterness smolder like ashes, and at times fan them into a full-blown blaze. This festering wound in our spirit can only be healed by forgiving that person.

We also use what another person (whether it is a family member, friend, boss, or a politician) has done to us as an excuse for our current behavior. I am not denying the pain and hurt we endured, but we are responsible for our behavior, despite how others act. When bad things were done to us as children, we did not know how to properly react. Now, as adults, we are responsible for our current behavior. Sometimes that involves forgiveness and restoration.

Definition of Forgiveness

Forgiveness is the act of setting someone free from an obligation to us that is a result of a wrong done to us. It also entails a commitment not to bring up again the wrong that was committed.

To fully understand forgiveness, it helps to know what it is not. It does not mean that what the person did was okay. It does not mean that with time the memory will go away (the pain will, but not the memory). It does not mean there won't be any consequences for the bad behavior.

Forgiveness is also not based upon our feelings. I hear many people say, "I'm not ready to forgive that person." They're waiting for their feelings to tell them that it's okay. Those feelings rarely come. Even in the midst of the tremendous hurt we may be going through, we must forgive the person who hurt us now.

Our hurt will be healed by our forgiving that person and moving on with our own life, not by our withholding forgiveness.

Types of Forgiveness and the Process

We want to hang on to the memories and let our feelings fester to their fullest fit of turmoil. We want the other person to pay for their mistake. However, reality shows that *we* are the ones who suffer, while the other person hasn't a clue of how hurt we are over the situation. Part of this healing process is learning to forgive.

Forgiving Others

Forgiveness is a choice. It's a decision we make based upon our desire to improve our life, not based upon our feelings. If we wait until we feel like forgiving people, we may never forgive. How soon after an event are we to forgive? Immediately. However, we don't immediately forget the event when others hurt us, but we can learn to allow the painful emotion to lessen over time.

Forgiveness is a process. Once we make the initial decision to forgive someone, we must decide whether we need to verbally tell that person we forgive them, or whether our internal decision is sufficient. This decision will be determined by the individuals involved and the circumstances. Dealing with our personal emotional pain should not bring additional emotional pain to others.

After our act of forgiveness, when the memories surface, we must immediately remind ourselves we have forgiven that person. We are to stop our thought process from rehashing the event and stirring our emotions into a frenzy. This thought process is where most people enjoy replaying the event in their mind and allowing themselves to feel justified for their reactions (both mentally and physically) to the hurt. Some don't want to let go of the memory and the hurt. They want to hold it as an ace for when that person hurts them again, then they can recall *all* instances of hurt to attack the person. Sound familiar spouses?

This process is not easy nor is it a one-time event. Sometimes it takes years for the pain from the memories to completely go away. Note: I didn't say the memories will go away. Hopefully, the memories stir us to become better people because of what happened to us and the lessons we learned from them.

What we turn our thoughts toward is important. Instead of dwelling upon other problems we may have, our goal is to direct our energy toward our future. Involvement in a project big enough to immerse ourselves in is what we're looking for.

Seeking Forgiveness

When we become aware that we have hurt someone, we are to go to that person as soon as possible and ask that person to forgive us.

This perspective differs from the above section on forgiving others. In that scenario, a person has hurt us and has not asked us for forgiveness. Here is a scenario under this section that we may not recognize: as a child, our parents did something that caused us great pain, and over the years we developed bitterness toward our parents. This bitterness now affects our relationship with our parents. As an adult, we are to forgive the things done to us as a child. Depending upon our relationship with our parents, we need to ask our parents for forgiveness for the bitterness we have or had toward them. However, if doing so would make things worse (i.e., they are unaware you are bitter toward them, nor do they know why), then it may not be a good idea to verbally tell them you forgive them. It helps to write out your request for forgiveness, detailing the reasons, so you can get it out of your mind for good, and then tear up the paper.

Forgiving Ourselves

What I see a lot of today is not giving or receiving forgiveness and staying stuck in the realm of feeding upon our guilt and also the sympathy we get from others. We enjoy our pity-parties. However, they lead to self-hatred every time we try to do better and we fail. We are the hardest person on ourselves. It's time to stop looking at the negative and start living in the positive. Forgiving ourselves is the first step to let go of this bondage we find ourselves in.

Restoring Relationships

After forgiveness has been given or received, we are to take the initiative to restore broken relationships. It's up to the other person whether he or she will accept our attempt at reconciliation. A lot of time should not elapse between the time of the hurtful event, our forgiveness, and our attempts at reconciliation. The more time allowed to pass, the harder hearts become—both ours and the other person's.

Restoration efforts should have the proper motivation and attitude. We are to lay aside our selfish desires and to love others unconditionally. Thus, our motivation is to put others ahead of our own desires. Because of our right motivation and our outpouring of our love, miracles can happen.

Hindrances to Forgiving

If you feel like something inside is stopping you from seeking forgiveness, review the following hindrances and see if any of them apply to you.

Pride. Forgiving others may make us appear to be weak.

We also enjoy the attention and sympathy we receive from others who know we've been wronged.

Control. We want to make sure the person is punished, in case God forgets. We won't release the person into God's hands.

Ignorance. We've not been taught how to respond to hurts and painful situations. We find it difficult to forgive because we haven't experienced others forgiving us.

The Keys to Forgiving

One of the keys to a forgiving spirit is to see the freedom it will bring us, and perhaps a restoration of the relationship.

A second key is that we have to want to change. We must want to rid ourselves of the guilt, allow peace to fill us and then move on with our life.

Results of Forgiveness

When we think of forgiving others we usually don't think of the benefits and how our life will be changed for the better.

Freedom from bondage. We have instant freedom from our internal turmoil. Our bitterness is gone. We don't feel tied to our past any longer.

Pain from memories begins to fade. As we let go of our grip on the past, the pain from our memories begins to fade. As the pain lessens, we spend less time dwelling upon our past.

We see the forgiven person in a different light. We can slowly change how we feel towards the person we forgave.

Possible reconciliation. Relationships now have the freedom to grow and develop into healthy, loving relationships.

As you can see from the above, forgiveness is something we must do to get rid of the bitterness, resentment and anger. This is something we must do daily, even for the small things that people do that affect us.

Tapping Through The Process

A great tool to help us through this process is to use Tapping at the same time. We can be by ourselves and we can be Tapping while we verbally forgive a person. This Tapping will help us let go of our emotions attached to that person or event.

Appendix C

Discover Your Passion

> *Passionate living is the lever to bring life and excitement into boring and meaningless lives.*
> ~ Kathy Williamson

The words of Martin Luther King, Jr. "I have a dream ..." changed the course of history forever. These four simple words can inspire change in ourselves, in others, a nation and the world. But until each of us can stand and proclaim "I have a dream ...," our life remains void of the abundant life we're seeking.

To overcome the vice grip that grief, overwhelming emotions, and fear of the unknown have on us, a stronger motivation must be found then just survival. The motivation of wanting things to just return to normal will not work in this pandemic that has destroyed what *normal* is. It is time to create a new normal in each of our lives which hopefully positively impacts our loved ones, friends, neighbors, our local community, and maybe even the world.

However, an additional problem has developed while

living in these uncertain times. Our mindset has become saturated with a focus on nothing but *me, myself and I*. This inward focus is extremely strong and difficult to overcome. Most of us aren't aware we have this problem.

To engage in passionate living means to use your passion in life as an avenue to reach out to love and help others. This results in resolving many problems:

- The inward focus of me, myself, and I.
- Provides a strong motivation to keep headed in the right direction.
- Gives us something to switch our thoughts and words toward when our emotions overwhelm us.
- Provides hope for an awesome future!

Have you ever had the experience of helping someone and by time you left that person or the situation you felt like you were more blessed than the person you helped? That is the motivation that keeps a person on track with their new lifestyle. When you add the element of actively engaging in one's passion in life, the motivation goes to an all-time high level and it pulls you into your new future.

It is time for you to take your dreams off the shelf and start living them. First, let's look at what *passionate living* is. I use the terms *passion, purpose,* and *vision* interchangeably.

Passionate Living

Passion is our heart's desire to make a difference somewhere, using our gifts and talents. Each of us has a unique passion. Most people have never identified their passion or even know if they have one. Passion can be classified into three general categories, although some overlap exists.

1. A passion about people. You long to make a difference in certain people's lives.
2. Operating in certain roles or functions. You receive

enormous enjoyment by your functioning in a certain role.
3. You have a passion for a cause, whether it is addressing the needs of world hunger, fighting against human trafficking, supporting politics, reaching the spiritually lost, etc.

While your passion may be to do a certain thing, look to the whole picture of what the ultimate outcome will be. An example of a person who has a passion to operate in a certain role or function might be someone who likes to help in whatever way they can; it can be as a visionary or a leader, or it can be as a member of a team that accomplishes the overall dream.

Identifying Your Passion

If you can't identify your passion right now, don't worry. The following exercise will assist you in the process. Get your pen and paper ready as you look through these six indicators to help you identify your passion.

1. *It impacts your daily routine.* When you talk about your passion, you speak a little faster, your body language changes in that you lean forward and your voice goes up a little. Your thoughts create emotions about your passion and drive you to stay up late at night or bounce out of bed early in the morning. What topic makes you react in this manner?
2. *You dream about it.* In your daydreaming you allow your heart's desire to take over and dream of things that don't currently exist, obstacles are removed, and your potential is unlimited. Your feelings get heightened and you know an emotional chord has been struck. What do you daydream about?
3. *Past achievements indicate themes.* Looking at your past achievements will indicate what you enjoy doing. This pattern helps you identify specific topics or ways of

relating, whether you're a leader, a follower, a planner, cause-oriented, task-oriented or people-oriented. Note: prior careers may not be your passion. What are the patterns of achievements which you enjoyed doing?

4. *Time passes quickly.* You're involved in a project or talking to people about a topic and suddenly you realize time has slipped away. What areas are you involved in where this happens?

5. *You have an inner confidence you are headed in the right direction.* When you are headed in the direction of your passion, no matter what obstacles you encounter, you are confident you are doing what you were born to do. What area are you involved in where you have confidence that you are headed in the right direction?

6. *Your passion energizes you.* Ever notice how much more physical and emotional energy you have when you're doing something you thoroughly enjoy? This is one way of identifying what your passion is. What things do you do where you recognize an increase in energy?

After reviewing your responses to these six factors, can you state in one or two sentences what your passion is? If you cannot identify your passion, ask a close friend to review these questions with you and provide insight.

You may find you enjoy doing many things and have a variety of gifts and natural talent. I challenge you to narrow the description of your passion into one area. The things that make your passion unique are your life experiences to date, your personality traits, and the natural talents you have. Now, what specific thing do you feel your passion in life is?

Capturing Your Vision.

You must dream big dreams; dreams so big that they require the help of others to make them happen. Once you know what your big dream is, you must break it down into manageable chunks. You must first recognize your dream, plan for it, and finally take action to implement it.

Have you spent time dreaming about how your passion to do certain activities can be put into a life-long vision? The complete picture may not be revealed all at once. Usually you only have the initial revelation of the vision for your life. The specifics come as you take each step when it's revealed.

Perhaps the idea of having a vision which guides and energizes you for the rest of your life is new to you. But that is exactly how God created you. If you've never thought along these lines, take time to consider what you would do with the rest of your life if you had no financial limitations or other restrictions. To help initiate dreaming, this exercise may help.

1. Write out everything you ever dreamed of doing. Things that are specific to you, not you and a spouse. If you are single, avoid "If I had a spouse, I would ..." Also avoid, "My only desire is to be married and raise a family, etc." The desire for a spouse is not something you can fulfill. But the dreams within you *can* be brought to realization.
2. Specifically identify the mental pictures your dreams produce.
3. Identify and feel the emotions you envision encountering as you carry out each step and eventually see your goals accomplished.

We were designed to do things as a team. Many of us need to change our dreams from "my" dream to "our" dream. All successful people have a team working with them. Remember, you can't do everything yourself—you weren't designed to do it all.

As you identify your passion and how you can turn it into

a lifelong goal to reach out to love and help others, create a vision board. This vision board will hold pictures of what your dream looks like in real life. You can search through magazines or pictures on the Internet to find the ones that represent your dream. If you cannot find pictures, then write out the words and put them on your board. For example, characteristics fall into this category: trustworthy, confident, reliable, giver, loyal, encourager, helper, etc. I suggest you create a vision board for things you wish to accomplish in the next year.

Keep Your Dream Fueled

How will you keep your dream fueled? You can't stay on an emotional high experience forever. When you encounter some confrontations, or your own flesh wants to rebel, what will you do to keep yourself committed to your dream and staying on the right path?

Keep your life in balance. Once we start working on our vision, we are so on-fire that we run off and start doing things 24/7. Because we receive such an immense high from this, we tend to continue working when we should be resting. We must maintain balance in our life to avoid burnout. When we receive opposition to our dreams, we must have people in our lives with whom we can talk to about what's happening, people who continue to encourage us to live up to the potential inside us.

Keep your thoughts right. Our thoughts are borne from our beliefs. We must stand on our belief that we were given this unique vision to carry. Once we stay committed to our vision, we must do something to propel us forward. Earlier we learned we can't go on the outside where we haven't gone on the inside. Therefore, we must spend time thinking about the vision, determining how to accomplish it, what the end results will look like, and what our emotions will be at each phase of the project. The more time spent meditating upon your dream and adding emotions to your mental picture and thinking, the more you will be motivated to stay on track. Sometimes it helps to write your thoughts on paper to quickly grab and meditate over them when things get rough. I encourage you to review your written vision every morning and evening.

Be accountable. Find someone whom you can share your dream with and also meet with on a weekly basis. You will probably have to ask someone to be your accountability partner. I have found that when I ask someone to be my accountability partner, they feel honored to do this. Choose a person whom you trust and know that they have your best interest in their heart. Give your partner permission to ask you the hard questions and you must be honest when you share your triumphs and struggles.

Cultivate faithfulness through obedience. This is a daily journey and we must recognize that we are only required to take the step before us. If we are not obedient, then we get stalled in our progress of carrying out our dream. If we're not going forward, we're going backward. We cannot stay in neutral! On days when we don't *feel* like taking action, that is when we must take action. Then our feelings come afterwards.

Stay focused. We are so easily sidetracked. Have you had times where you seemed to get a lot done in a short period of time, even though you had that same opportunity day after day? You got a lot done because you were intensely focused. You didn't let anything interrupt what you were doing until you got that job done. The same holds true for staying on track with your dream. You must purposely determine to stay focused. You may need to inform others around you not to interrupt you for a period of time because you want to get a particular thing done.

Work or Volunteer?

What do you do if your vision has nothing to do with your current job? The ideal situation is to be able to work at doing what you are passionate about. Since this may not happen immediately, research where you can volunteer where you can use your passion. Then when society lifts the restrictions due to COVID-19, you will be ready to take immediate, positive action.

Through volunteering you gain the experience of putting together the pieces of the puzzle that comprise your dream. It allows you to determine what skills you need to develop or what education you need. It allows you the time to improve yourself so that when the doors open for you to get paid doing this full time, you are ready.

One thing that helps me a lot is to volunteer during the times I find myself most vulnerable to sit and do nothing and start to go downhill. For me as a single person it is Saturday nights and Sunday afternoons. Since I volunteered at Christian-based crisis hotlines, I could choose almost any five-hour shift I wanted. When are your most vulnerable times?

You'll be amazed at how many volunteer opportunities exist in your community. Look on the Internet, ask at your church, or call the United Way or other volunteer organizations in your county and find a place where you can volunteer once a week. Any lesser amount of time will not keep you focused and involved. Even if you don't think you have the skills or education, call and find out in what capacity you can volunteer. Being around others in the field that interests you will motivate you. This process is also good for family members who are old enough to volunteer. This time away from the chaos in your home will greatly benefit you. Being around people in person will breathe fresh air into your life.

If you don't know what your passion is, don't wait until you have all the answers. Volunteering gives you the opportunity to try many different avenues to help you determine what you are passionate about. When you find that area, start meditating to see how to create the big vision for you.

Don't ignore what you are learning at your day job. Many principles you need to learn can be learned while working at your job. While your vision may eventually become your career, your current job is your pre-occupation until doors open for you to make that move.

Shift Your Focus to 80/20

During this time of isolation and possibly living in emotional overwhelm, you may be spending a lot of time rehashing your hurts, anger and rage, how frustrated you are because of the impact of COVID-19 in your daily life. and wondering if circumstances will ever change for the better. Remember that whatever picture is inside your mind, is what will materialize in your outer circumstances. Playing games on your phone or computer is not helping you move forward I life.

Now that you have discovered your passions in life, you have something to shift your focus to. The goal is to spend 80% of your thought life and actions focusing on building your awesome future, and spend 20% of your time working on maintaining your emotional stability and/or resolving any underlying issues you may have.

I would suggest the first step is for you to add up the number of hours you spend each week (1) texting, (2) watching TV, (3) surfing the Internet or reviewing emails, (4) reading newspapers, magazines or novels, or (5) any other activity of distraction, and use that time to focus on building your awesome future. However, family time should be kept in your schedule.

Make a list of the areas of your life that can be replaced

with working on building your awesome future. Take time now to write out how you plan to go from where you are today to the point of achieving your vision. Then break it down to monthly, weekly and daily goals. Having these in writing will provide you with guidance of what to do when you get emotionally overwhelmed in trying to deal with the impact of COVID-19 pandemic on you and society.

You might wonder how you could ever make this drastic change in your schedule and stick to it. You will find that after the first day of doing this, you will have such a peace and calm inside you, that you will be drawn back to repeat this in every spare moment you have. Why? Because when a person is operating within their passion, they get so excited, that they can't wait to come back and do it again. Fulfillment and significance begin to permeate their soul. When I started operating within my passion, I enjoyed the "high" I got from living in this realm, and was able to turn my life around in three to four months and never go back to my former lifestyle.

If you don't know what your passion is at this moment, you need to discover something that you thoroughly enjoy doing and begin to do that. You must find something to switch your focus to that will enable you to start creating your life, even during these uncertain times.

As time goes on, if you find yourself in emotional overwhelm or boredom, you should take a look at your schedule and you might notice that you have gotten off of this 80/20 schedule.

Appendix D

Daily Rituals

Morning

1. Read my daily affirmations (new beliefs to reduce emotions / to instill hope for my future) while Tapping.
2. Anybody I didn't forgive yesterday? Forgive them now.
3. Review and visualize myself doing my main goal today that will propel me into fulfilling my vision.
4. Visualize myself accomplishing my vision. What are my feelings, emotions? Whose lives did I impact? Review your Vision Board.
5. What kind of involvement can I intentionally have today with my family/friends?
6. How can I intentionally show love and encouragement to others today? What specific actions or words will I use?
7. Review my planner for the activities scheduled for today.

Evening

1. Review how well I handled my emotions today. How could I handle some of them differently in the future?

What were the thoughts behind the emotions? What different thoughts can I use in the future to avoid becoming negative?

2. Is there anybody I need to forgive for what was said or done to me today? Forgive them now.

3. Do I need to reach out to ask for forgiveness from someone I might have hurt today? If so, when will I do that (specific date/time)?

4. Did I accomplish my one main goal today? If not, what thoughts or excuses kept me from doing it?

5. What thoughts or inactions do I need to do Tapping on? Do it now.

6. What am I grateful for in my life in general and from today's activities?

7. What is one main goal (personal or business) for tomorrow that will make me be excited when I wake up? Visualize myself doing the actions to carry it out.

Appendix E

Resources

Canfield, Jack and Bruner, Pamela *Tapping Into Ultimate Success: How to Overcome Any Obstacle and Skyrocket Your Results*, U.S.: Hay House, Inc., 2013.

Canfield, Jack and Switzer, Janet *The Success Principles: How to Get from Where You Are to Where You Want to Be*, U.S. HarperCollins Publishers, 2005.

Chapman, Gary *Love Language Minute for Couples: 100 Days to a Closer Relationship*, Tyndale Momentum, 2019.

Chapman, Gary *The 5 Love Languages: The Secret to Love that Lasts*, Chicago: Northfield Publishing, 2015.

Chapman, Gary and Pellicane, Arlene *Growing Up Social: Raising Relational Kids in a Screen-Driven World*, Chicago: Northfield Publishing, 2014 New Edition.

Church, Dawson, Ph.D. *EFT for PTSD,* California: Energy Psychology Press, 2014.

Church, Dawson, Ph.D. *The EFT Manual*, California: Energy Psychology Press, 2018 4th Edition

Elrod, Hal, *The Miracle Equation: Unwavering Faith & Extraordinary Effort = Miracles*, New York: Harmony Books, 2019.

Foster, Jan K. *The Tapping Spy: Uncovering Emotional Freedom Techniques (EFT Tapping) for Kids*, True Potential, Inc., 2020.

Lynch, Margaret M. with Schwartz, Daylle Deanna *Tapping Into Wealth: How EFT Can Help You Clear the Path to Making More Money*, TarcherPerigee, 2014

Ortner, Alex, *Gorilla Thumps & Bear Hugs: A Tapping Solution Children's Story,* U.S.: Hay House, Inc., 2016.

Ortner, Nick *The Tapping Solution: A Revolutionary System for Stress-Free Living,* U.S.: Hay House, 2014, 8th Edition.

Smith, Sherrie Rice, R.N. (Retire), *EFT For Christians Advanced: Change Your Feelings, Change Your Life*, True Potential, Inc., 2017.

Wommack, Andrew, *A Better Way to Pray: If your prayer life is not working, consider hanging directions,* Harrison House, Inc., 2007.

Wommack, Andrew, *God Wants You Well: What the Bible Really Says About Walking in Divine Health*, Harrison House, Inc., 2010.

Wommack, Andrew, *Harnessing Your Emotions*, Harrison House, Inc., 2012.

Wommack, Andrew *The Believer's Authority: What you didn't learn in church* (available through author's website www.AWMI.net.

Wommack, Andrew, *You've Already Got It! (So Quite Trying To Get It)*, Harrison House, Inc., 2009.

Websites

Andrew Wommack, Bible Teacher – https://AWMI.net

EFT for Christians – https://EFTForChristians.com

Kids Learn EFT Tapping –

https://KidsLearnEFTTapping.com

The Tapping Solution (Nick Ortner) –

https://www.TheTappingSolution.com

The Tapping Solution App (Nick Ortner) –

https://www.TheTappingSolutionApp.com

Veterans EFT Tapping Project –

http://www.VeteransEFTTappingProject.org

Veterans Stress Project – https://StressProject.org

Welcome Home Vets

http://www.WelcomeHomeVets.org

Kathy E. Williamson
Author, Speaker & Trainer

Kathy Williamson created the Roadmaps To Freedom™ series of books. The first book in this series is Emotional Freedom From COVID-19: How to Stop the Overwhelm, Build a New Life ... and Beat the Odds!

Each of the books sets forth her "7 C's to Transformation That Sticks" process. Kathy began creating this process after she got out of her ten-year addiction back in 1990 and perfected it while writing her recent couple of books:

- *My Friend Is An Addict – What Can I Do? Use the Roadmap Out of Addiction to Influence the Addict and To Take Back Your Life (2018)* (paperback and eBook available on Amazon).
- *Tapping Away Your Addiction: Freedom and Confidence in Yourself Await You, (2018)* helps addicts use the Tapping technique to control their emotions so they can recover from their addictions and stop relapsing (eBook available on Amazon).

Having lived both the life of being an addict for 10 years, plus being married to a narcissist who sucked the life out of her (but she got her life back), she provides a unique approach to help many people get unstuck from their problems.

During the COVID-19 pandemic Kathy had a good friend pass away (unrelated to the virus). During that time she was unable to visit her friend to say goodbye or attend the service for her friend. This led to overwhelming grief, on top of all the other stresses from living in a pandemic in the U.S. Kathy applied her own process to her life while grieving, and the overwhelming emotions were reduced, which allowed her to carry on with her daily activities.

Kathy brings hope and healing to thousands struggling with their emotions. Her background as a lay counselor on hotlines for over 13 years brings wisdom and insights as to what causes struggles in life and how to get over them.

As a Christian since 1980, Kathy brings biblical principles into her work, although not necessarily using religious terminology. She believes that these principles work, regardless of whether a person has a relationship with God.

Kathy will continue writing more books in her *Roadmaps To Freedom* series. These topics include:

- Teach addicts how to stop the relapse cycle and create a great life
- Help Christians integrate their faith to take bold actions to rise to a new level of living
- Provide guidance to help people take control of their health when doctors cannot provide solutions
- ... and more

To contact Kathy Williamson, please write, email or call:
Kathy Williamson
KW Consulting & Training, LLC
dba Roadmaps to Freedom
P.O. Box 10305
Prescott, AZ 86304
Kathy@EmotionalFreedomFromCOVID19.com
(877) 364-2424